FRIEND

The Story of George Fox and the Quakers

BY JANE YOLEN

FOREWORD BY LARRY INGLE

Quaker Press
OF FRIENDS GENERAL CONFERENCE
PHILADELPHIA, PENNSYLVANIA

PLACES IMPORTANT IN GEORGE FOX'S LIFE

N

SCOTLAND

NORTH SEA

IRELAND

Carlisle

WESTMORLAND

RAWTHEY R.

Ulverston
SWARTHMORE HALL

Sedbergh
PENDLE HILL
Lancaster

Scarborough

YORKSHIRE

IRISH SEA

MORECAMBE BAY

Preston

Patrington

ENGLAND

Mansfield

Derby

Nottingham

LEICESTERSHIRE

Lichfield

Mancetter

Leicester

WALES

Fenny Drayton

Warwick

Worcester

Oxford

Whetstone

THE BRITISH ISLES

Bristol

Reading

London

Launceston

Ives

ENGLISH CHANNEL

STATUTE MILES
0   50   100

KILOMETERS
0   50   100   150

FRANCE
A.M. JAUSS

For the Friends of Acton Meeting
Acton, Massachusetts

ISBN-10: 1-888305-41-X
ISBN-13: 978-1-888305-41-8

First edition published by The Seabury Press, New York, NY, 1972.

Second edition published by Quaker Press of Friends General Conference, Philadelphia, PA, 2005.

Library of Congress Cataloging-in-Publication Data
Yolen, Jane.
   Friend : the story of George Fox and the Quakers / by Jane Yolen ; foreword by Larry Ingle. — 2nd ed.
      p. cm.
   Includes bibliographical references and index.
   ISBN-13: 978-1-888305-41-8
      1. Fox, George, 1624–1691—Juvenile literature.   2. Quakers—Great Britain—Biography—Juvenile literature.   3. Quakers—Biography—Juvenile literature.
   I. Title.
   BX7795.F7Y65   2005
   289.6092—dc22
                                    2005029485

Picture credits:

   Art object (front and back cover):
      Unidentified artist, British, 18th century or first quarter 19th century, British. *Quaker Meeting* (detail). Oil on canvas. Museum of Fine Arts, Boston. Bequest of Maxim Karolik. Photograph © 2005 Museum of Fine Arts, Boston

   Picture of George Fox (front cover): Print by Robert Spence of George Fox courtesy of the Library of the Religious Society of Friends in Britain. It is part of a collection of 191 prints by Spence mostly illustrating Fox's *Journal* and other episodes from early Quakerism.

   Map (p. ii) by Anne Marie Jauss.

Special thanks to:

   Bob Lyon of the Cambridge AFSC and his wife Pat, for reading the manuscript from a Friend's point of view;

   Virginia Corwin of the Smith College Department of Religion, old mentor, old friend, for her comments and criticisms;

   Jim Giblin and Laura Kassos of The Seabury Press for serving as my second (and third) pair of eyes;

   and always David Stemple, my husband and my best friend.

Cover design and composition by David Budmen.

For further information about this publication
and other Quaker resources, please contact:

   Friends General Conference
   1216 Arch Street, 2B
   Philadelphia, PA 19107
   215-561-1700
   Or find us at www.fgcquaker.org

To order this or other publications call 800-966-4556

E-mail: bookstore@fgcquaker.org

You can order from us on the web at www.quakerbooks.org

Contents

Foreword   *vii*

Author's Note   *xi*

Prologue: Meeting   *3*

1: The Birth of Silence 1624–1643   7

2: The Seeker 1643–1646   *17*

3: The First Ministry 1646–1650   24

4: A Year in Derby Jail 1650–1651   *33*

5: The Man in Leather Breeches 1651   *42*

6: Meeting the Fells 1652   *52*

7: The Word Is Spread 1653   *60*

8: Meeting Oliver Cromwell 1653–1654   *68*

9: Doomsdale 1655–1656   *76*

10: The Fall of James Nayler 1656   *88*

11: The Return of the King 1658–1660   *98*

12: Restoration—the Renewal of Persecution
    1661–1664   *107*

13: The Longest Imprisonment 1663–1666   *114*

14: United in the Seed 1667–1671   *124*

15: America 1671–1673   *137*

16: Schism 1673–1678   *147*

17: Death and Transfiguration 1678–1691   *158*

Epilogue: Quakers Today   *164*

Bibliography   *173*

Index   *177*

Foreword

First published more than thirty years ago, this brief biography of George Fox, principal founder of the Quakers, will be welcomed by a new, and youthful, audience. Its author, Jane Yolen, who has written numerous children's books, now has grown children of her own; perhaps her grandchildren will now find this edition inviting

Like most books designed for a young readership *Friend: The Story of George Fox and the Quakers* was not based on original research. Instead, it drew its facts and interpretations from published works. Where it did rely on what scholars call primary documents, it used that most basic one, Fox's own *Journal*, which was first published in 1694, three years after its author's death. But it gave Fox's own recollections, something that anyone who tries to remember exactly what happened last week should be wary of. More on this point later.

Inevitably, Jane Yolen's book reflected the findings of historical research of the time—indeed, a little before 1972 when it was published. I say a little before because one of the scholars she used most, the renowned Rufus Jones, was already under something of a cloud, one that had enshrouded him for nearly two decades before she wrote. Safe to say, that darkness has not disappeared to this day, more than fifty years since. Hence most modern writers today would not describe Quakerism, as Yolen, following Jones, does, as a third form of Christianity (p. 165).

No one can be blamed, of course, for not knowing what no one else knows at any given time. We all stand on the shoulders of those who have gone before us; we can hardly leap over them, to know what bountiful knowledge unfolds in the future. Jane Yolen was writing for her time when she wrote in 1972, and she was writing her time, too.

More than twenty years after Yolen wrote, in 1994, I also published a biography of George Fox. Its title is *First Among Friends: George Fox and the Creation of Quakerism.* It was the first one to go a long way beyond the source materials that he wanted us to have, those contained in his *Journal* and other collected writings. I unearthed a lot of things that no one else had looked for. Moreover, I tried to glimpse the context of his life; that is, I examined the circumstances that surrounded the events he described and left us records of in his writings. My interest in context was like aiming a flashlight and shinning it around a darkened room, full of the happenings in his life. I did not find everything, for no one, no matter how skilled, can totally recreate the past. Suddenly, though, things popped out, things that influenced and affected Fox's decisions. Now we can see some of the other things around him that interested and provoked Fox. The things Fox recalled when he dictated *Journal* in the 1670s were those that were at the top of his mind. All such memories are somewhat self-serving.

They seek to explain and perhaps defend the person who is remembering, and they present that person's version of events; any omissions send signals of what the author prefers to be overlooked or forgotten. Such documents have to be used with care, lest they distort the picture we receive.

Needless to say, Jane Yolen would have written a somewhat different book after 1994 than she did in 1972. Let me mention only one example: on pages 18 and 19, she writes of Fox's wanderings when he was a teenager of nineteen. He stayed on the road and away from home for more than six months, traveling around the countryside; he ended up in London, nearly 100 miles from his home in rural southern Leicestershire. But Yolen does not mention something else that was happening at the time, something that was tearing the nation apart. (She gets around to barely mentioning it to her readers on page 40.) I am referring to a war that was being fought in the very region where Fox had grown to age nineteen, where churches were being invaded, and people slaughtered. Here, she does not label it for what it was, a bitter civil war that set family against family and tore into fragile communities in the area. Nor does she inform us that of the four towns Fox visited on his way to London, two of them contained large garrisons of parliamentary army—soldiers of the same age as the young Fox.

Our nineteen-year-old was himself a prime candidate for what was called the "New Model Army" of preaching and praying soldiers. He likely chose to linger in Northampton and Newport Pagnell to see how youths of his own age were making out as troopers. Nor does she explore the mental depression that caught up with Fox at one town, Barnet, just north of London. He spent a page and a half of his *Journal* pouring out the details of the stresses that kept him in his room or walking fitfully in the fields, searching for answers to problems that were literally wearing him down. Yolen, like most writers before her, was more interested in religion and decided to skip over this troubling and painful psychological episode.

Every writer makes errors, and Jane Yolen does too. Some are relatively minor—like the one on page 53 where she makes the priest of the Fells' parish a kinsman of theirs—but another was more serious. On page 105, she has Fox write a private letter to King Charles II in which he supposedly announced the peace testimony a year before it was written by Fox and Richard Hubberthorne, another leading Friend. And four pages later (and again on page 170), she assigns the 1661 testimony to Fox's pen alone, leaving out co-author Hubberthorne.

Such errors aside, Jane Yolen has still given young readers a delightful and always readable introduction to Fox, if not always to his times. Her selection of quotations is creative, and she uses them in a way to make him live, not only as a historical figure but also one who has something to say to our own times. Torn by war and wracked by uncertainty and doubt, the people of Fox's age wanted answers, and our author demonstrates those he offered. Especially useful is her depiction of Fox after about 1660 when he turned his attention to stabilizing the Quaker movement so it could withstand the persecution that descended on its members.

So read this book and gain a renewed appreciation of a man who, as his follower William Penn wrote, tried to "revive primitive Christianity" and give it meaning to the lives of a new generation. You are part of another new generation, and, if you are a Quaker, you can help make it flourish on into the future as it has for more than 350 years. Quaker or not, perhaps you will be inspired also to go beyond it and explore the richness existing in other writers' depictions of George Fox's life and faith.

LARRY INGLE

Author's Note

George Fox was a man of his time. His ideas, radical as they were, were shaped by the peculiar religious, political, and social climate of seventeenth century England. Yet, though he was a product of the 1600s, he has much to say to us today.

Fox was a militant pacifist, a man of such moral convictions that he refused to be drafted to fight in his own country's Civil War. He would bow to no man, considering all men equal. He spoke out against the conditions of prisons and the low place of women in society. He wore strange clothes, would not cut his hair, and spoke a language peculiar to his beliefs. And he did all these things, though imprisoned and beaten for them, even threatened with death. George Fox was not afraid to "speak truth to power."

If, as Peter Marin, the contemporary teacher and writer, suggests, every *sensitive* man experiences in himself the conflicts and contradictions of his age, then it is easy to call George Fox a sensitive man. And if, as Marin further states, the *great* man is the one who articulates and resolves these conflicts in a way that has meaning for himself and others, then it can not be denied that George Fox was a great man.

George Fox lived from 1624 to 1691, but his spirit lives today. His message of the Inner Light and the brotherhood of men is as timely now as when he first cried it in the wildernesses of England. It is a message with which the young people of today are particularly in tune.

JANE YOLEN

He was an original, being no man's copy.
—WILLIAM PENN

What I am in words, I am the same in life.
—GEORGE FOX

An institution is the lengthened shadow
of one man; as . . . Quakerism, of Fox.
—RALPH WALDO EMERSON

There syllabled by silence, let me hear
The still small voice which reached the prophet's ear.
                              —JOHN GREENLEAF WHITTIER

Prologue

Meeting

This simple building holds a silence. It is a silence that is often heard in nature. On a mountainside at dawn, before the birds begin their morning calls, you can hear this silence. In a stream before the water rushes over rocks, you can hear it. In a pine forest, with the sun shining down and warming you, if you close your eyes and think of nothing at all, you will hear this silence.

The silence is very strong and, strangely, very loud.

This simple building holds that silence. It is a place where the Friends, or Quakers, worship. It is called a Meeting House.

Come inside. Here are rows of pews, ancient seats of

fragrant wood. They are stiff and upright but beautiful, very much like the seventeenth century Quaker fathers. Sunlight streams across the aisles from plain untinted windows. Instead of an altar, there are benches in front facing the pews. This is where the Elders of the Meeting sit. There are no ornaments, no stained glass windows or gold finishings in this place of worship. Yet the simplicity possesses a beauty that is all the more striking.

We are the first inside. Already the silence has caught us. Let us sit down. But quietly.

Others are coming now. They also slip quietly into their seats, smiling, nodding at their neighbors. There is a sense of community here, a coming together. Some of the people bow their heads. Others look up, around. Some of the Elders are entering, too. Despite their title, they are not all old. Some are young, new mothers and fathers; or middle-aged. They do not march in solemnly, full of pride in their position. They come in the way we entered, quietly, so as to enter into the silent communion with the other Friends.

Now the Meeting House is filled with people. There is a settling down as each person finds his or her way into the silence.

This is the hardest part of the Quaker meeting. See if you can enter into its spirit. First you must cut out the sounds of the world. Do you hear that bird chirping outside? Forget it for now. The fly buzzing at the window? Don't listen. The man next to you coughing? You haven't heard him.

Now there are no outside noises left. But there are inside ones. You remember some work you have left undone. Perhaps the name of someone you should call. Part of a funny story floats through your head. Slowly, with a great deal of effort, you must forget these inside noises, too. You have? Good.

Now you are ready. Your heart is open—open to God and to communion and to love. *"Love,"* say the Quakers, *"links us all across the sundering leagues. Love makes us brothers."*

You come back from your silence with a start. How long has it been? Seconds? Minutes? Perhaps even an hour has passed. It is not often that one can "center down" so easily. What has broken into your silent communion? Someone is speaking. It is one of the Elders. He is standing and talking of work and love. "Work," he says, quoting the poet Kahlil Gibran, "is love made visible." You think about that. You think about all he is saying and let it become incorporated in your silence again. Then someone else stands. It is not an Elder. It is a round-faced woman off to your left in a side row. She talks more about work, elaborates on the Elder's statement. She speaks of work as a loving sacrifice for God.

Perhaps someday you will feel called to speak, to say what has come to you in the deep inner silence of your heart. To share it with others. To make communion into community.

Then all is quiet again and you think about what the Elder and the woman have said. You try to relate what you have just heard to your life.

Suddenly, the Clerk of the Meeting reaches over and shakes his neighbor's hand. Everyone begins shaking the hands of his neighbors, his friends.

Meeting is over.

Many ministers and priests and rabbis use silent prayers in their services. But this meeting of silence, broken only when someone feels an inner call to speech, is different.

Is it new? How new? How did this unique and uniquely beautiful way of worshiping begin?

It began over three hundred years ago, in a little town in England called Drayton-in-the-Clay, or Fenny Drayton, with the birth of George Fox.

If George says Verily, there is
no altering him.
—GEORGE FOX, *Journal*

Chapter 1

The Birth of Silence

In the seventeenth century the western edge of Leicestershire was a narrow strip of swampy undrained land filled with bogs and low places. In that dank fen country, Christopher and Mary Fox lived in Drayton-in-the-Clay, a small hamlet nestled in the strip of land between the hills.

Christopher Fox, a weaver and warden of his church, was an exceedingly honest and upright man, called "Righteous Christer" by his neighbors. Since these were times of great individual involvement with religion, the fact that his friends gave him such a nickname meant that he was an especially pious person, even for the day.

Mary Lagos Fox, his wife, was of the "stock of martyrs." She had a number of ancestors who had been
burned at the stake for their religious convictions. She
was not just a simple weaver's wife, but "accomplished
above most of her degree," as a contemporary was
later to write, more educated and cultivated than the
poor villagers among whom she lived.

Their first son, George, was born in July 1624, and
grew up with four brothers and sisters in one of the
grass-roofed, one-hearth cottages of Drayton.

From the beginning, George was different from the
other village children. Though they all attended St.
Michael's Church in Drayton, only George seemed
really affected by it. He was much more solemn, less
playful, than his young friends. While they were interested in the loud, boisterous running games of child-
hood, George's mind was already turning inwards. By
the time he was eleven, young Fox had begun to judge
the adults by the way they treated their fellow men. If
he saw them dealing harshly with one another, with
little mutual respect, George would say, "If I ever
come to be a man, surely I shall not do so, nor be so
wanton." He was, as his friend William Penn would
write later, "from a child . . . religious, inward, still,
solid, and observing beyond his years."

Any other parents, seeing their son so grave and
pious—and being so religious themselves—would have
immediately apprenticed him to one of the many
priests in England. Since a weaver could not afford a
university education for his son, apprenticeship was

the only answer. And in the seventeenth century, a "priest" was any man who received money for preaching, whatever his education or religion. Priests were automatically assured a good living.

But Mary Fox showed a rare understanding of her son's gifts. When relatives urged that he be pushed into the ministry of the established church, Mary Fox resisted. Instead, she persuaded her husband to apprentice George to a shoemaker in the neighboring town of Mancetter. This shoemaker, George Gee, also dealt in wool and cattle.

By his own account, young George was a fine apprentice whose help "blessed" the shoemaker. Certainly Gee benefitted from George's reputation for honesty. As was commonly noted by the Mancetter folk, Fox's word was always good. They said, "If George says Verily, there is no altering him." As George's master, Gee profited from the boy's good name, and as long as George remained with him, his business flourished.

In Mancetter, George learned all the cobbling skills. But he spent more of his time with his master's sheep up in the Leicestershire hills. Years later, though Fox's contemporaries would often refer to him as a cobbler, it was the shepherding that he did for Gee that he remembered best. Many of his finest letters would be couched in shepherding terms. It was an employment that seemed perfect for George, both for its "innocency and solitude" and as a symbol of his later call to ministry. In the quiet, solemn hills, alone with Gee's sheep, the teen-age George Fox began his search for direct inner communion with God, a communion without benefit of church or clergy. In the silence of those Leicestershire hills, the Quaker silence was born.

What was it George discovered during his lonely shepherd's vigil, studying his Bible and opening his heart to God? To understand that, one must first understand the turmoil and upheavals going on in English and European churches during the hundred years before Fox was born.

The very fact that young George could read the Bible and attempt to reach God without an intermediary priest or church was made possible by the acts of a scholarly German monk and a volatile English king a century before George Fox was born.

The German priest was Martin Luther who, starting in 1517, protested what he saw as the excesses and corruption of the established Roman Catholic Church in Germany. Luther's rebellion grew into the religious movement known as the Reformation and led to the birth of Protestantism on the European continent.

The king was Henry VIII, Henry Tudor. In 1527, Henry was without a male heir and Catherine, who had been his wife for twenty-four years, was past childbearing. Henry's roving royal eye fell on Anne Boleyn, a spirited, beautiful noblewoman, as a possible successor to the queen. But Catherine and Henry were Catholic. And in the Catholic faith—which was England's state religion—divorce was unheard of, at least without the Pope's dispensation.

Because Catherine, a Spanish princess as well as Queen of England, did not want a divorce—and for other more political reasons as well—the Pope refused to dissolve the royal marriage. Henry then took a step which was unprecedented in English history. He declared himself the head of the English Church with the famous Act of Supremacy in 1534. He also declared, in a separate act, that the Pope had no authority in England. These two acts officially established the Reformation in England.

The new English Protestant Church was still very close to Roman Catholicism, but in England, for the first time, the head of the church and the head of the state were one. To deny King Henry's right to a divorce had now become a treasonable act for which a number of prominent church men paid with their lives. Henry divorced Catherine and married Anne Boleyn. But she was destined to be only his second wife. By the time Henry VIII died in 1547, he had divorced two wives, beheaded two (including Anne Boleyn), and outlived one. His last wife, Catherine Parr, outlived him.

When Henry cast off the Roman Catholic Church in 1534, the subsequent turmoil—both religious and political—served to pave the way for the mystical, righteous young boy who was to become the vibrant, hard-working, inspired spiritual leader, George Fox.

What did the casting off of the church mean? It meant that the common people for the first time had more of a voice in their own religion. It also meant that English money stayed in England and did not find its way into the pockets of foreign priests, something which had been disturbing the English for many years. And soon after Henry proclaimed himself divorced, an official English version of the Bible was placed in the parish churches.

This may not sound very exciting to us in the twentieth century, where Bibles in English can be found in every church, library, school, and hotel room. But until that time, very few English men and women had ever read the Bible which was the basis of their religion. The Bible had always been the special property of the educated priests and noblemen who could read Latin, the only language in which the Bible was printed. The first English version, by John Wycliffe, had been banned in 1384. In the next century, William Tyndale had been forced to leave England in order to finish his translation of the New Testament into English. But Tyndale had said to a friend, "If God spare my life, ere many years I will cause a boy that driveth the plough shall know more of the Scripture than thou dost."

The boy who drove a plough and his neighbors—the common people—at the time of Henry VIII's reign were suddenly given that Bible in their own language. Over the next hundred years, literacy expanded as the people learned to read with their Bibles. They became conversant with Scripture and a whole new world of thought and emotion was opened to them. Instead of having things interpreted by priests and lords, they could read, and read into, the Bible whatever they liked. This was a revolution that would have far-reaching effects.

After King Henry VIII died, his only son, the boy-king Edward VI, reigned briefly. It was during his reign that the great English prayer book was drawn up, yet another wedge in the ever-widening split between people and priests.

But Mary Tudor, the daughter of the divorced Queen Catherine, succeeded to the throne on Edward's death. Like her mother, Mary was a Catholic. She restored Catholicism to England for five bloody years. They were bloody because, among other things, Mary caused 300 obstinate Protestants to be burned at the stake.

Elizabeth I, Henry's daughter by Anne Boleyn and the great queen of English history, came to the throne next. With her came a compromise form of religious worship—Anglicanism. The queen was head of the church as her father had been, the services were in English, but the rituals were almost indistinguishable from those of Rome. Still, religious freedom was yet to become an English right. As one of Elizabeth's critics put it: "The right of free belief was granted; the right of free expression of that belief denied." Practicing Catholics were persecuted because, although people could think any way they wanted to, they were not allowed to do anything about it.

If England's Catholic neighbors had left well enough alone, the English common folk would probably have gone on for years with the same semi-freedom of religion. But the Catholic countries—especially Spain—tried to recruit Catholics against Elizabeth. In return, Elizabeth stepped up religious persecution, both against the Catholics and also against the Puritans who were trying to purify the English Protestant Church of its Romish practices.

James I, son of Mary, Queen of Scots, succeeded Elizabeth on the English throne in 1603. To further confuse matters, James was a Scottish Presbyterian, a dour Calvinist. To his reign's credit, we have the beautiful King James Bible, written at the time when most scholars agree the English language was at its poetic best. However, James felt bound to enforce church unanimity. Those church people who did not agree with the established church soon fled England. One of the groups that left was the Pilgrim fathers who settled in America.

Next to rule England was King Charles and his French Catholic queen, Henrietta Maria. Because of the queen, Catholicism became the court religion again.

With all this turning away from and returning to Catholicism by the English kings and queens, we might logically call the century between Henry VIII and Charles and Henrietta Maria *the weathercock years.* For the churchmen in England, out of fear for their goods, their jobs, even their lives, turned round and round between the Papish and Protestant Churches like weathercocks in a strong wind. William Penn,

looking back on that period, was to write: "Thousands
. . . lamentably perjured themselves four or five times
over. . . . In which sin the clergy transcended. . . ."

That is why many people in England, precursors of
George Fox, grew disgusted with the weathercocking
priests: priests who followed religiously only the religion that was currently in fashion.

The now common English Bible plus the turn-about
priests led to the formation of hundreds of independent
groups of worshipers with such marvelous names as
Familists, Brownists, Seekers, Adamists. And the fact
that the church on the European continent had already been divided in 1517 by Martin Luther and his
Reformation meant that the English Protestants did
not have to wrestle with a great measure of guilt for the
division. Luther had insisted that each Christian had
to do his own believing just as he had to do his own
dying. That thought would lead directly to the ideas of
George Fox.

Every ploughboy—and farmer and weaver and cobbler, too—now considered himself an expert on dogma.
It was as though arguing about theology had become
the national sport in England.

One contemporary writer described 176 "errors,
heresies [and] blasphemies," but this only covered the
lunatic fringes of the Protestant movement and did not
begin to count the divisions between the larger conservative groups like the Scottish Calvinists and the
Anglicans.

It was into this maelstrom of religious thought that

George Fox was born, less than a year before Charles I and Queen Henrietta Maria ascended the throne.

As a small child in a small village, he would probably have known little directly of this history as it was being made about him. Yet he could not help but be affected by the changes in the religious atmosphere. And when Fox was old enough to go up into the fen country hills with Gee's sheep, King Charles and his Catholic queen were setting the stage for persecuting the Pilgrims and other groups that searched for their own religious truths.

George Fox was born a seeker, and he was born into a seeking age.

> I was a man of sorrows in the time
> of the first workings of the Lord in me.
> —GEORGE FOX, *Journal*

Chapter 2

The Seeker

One day in 1643, when George Fox was a big-boned, broad-faced young man of nineteen, he went to the fair to do some business for Gee. At the bustling market-place, he met his cousin Bradford, a professor. A professor in the seventeenth century was anyone who was a church member. Bradford, a convivial sort, invited young Fox to share a jug of beer with him and a friend.

George was thirsty from his walk into town, and so gladly joined the two. They found a small tavern nearby. After a glass apiece, Fox was ready to leave. He had drunk simply to quench his thirst. But his companions were there for sport. They started drinking toasts and proposed a game in which the one who did not match the others drink for drink would pay for all.

Taking a coin from his pocket, George put it on the table and rose, saying, "If it be so, I'll leave you."

It was a common enough incident. Yet somehow it shocked Fox so completely he could not forget it. That two professors were so "wanton" and "light" seemed terribly wrong. George believed that food and drink were given by God for the health of the body, not to addle men's minds or make them greedy and self-indulgent. Instead of simply dismissing the incident from his mind as a day's foolishness, Fox went home and spent the night in pacing and praying.

In the middle of the night, he suddenly had a vision. In it, God spoke to him and said: "Thou seest how young people go together into vanity, and old people into the earth; thou must forsake all, young and old, keep out of all, and be as a stranger unto all."

It was a call to solitary wandering. George Fox answered that call. On November 9, 1643, he broke off from his family, left his trade, and went out into the world to see if he could discover from the priests and professors the true religion by which an honest and humble person might live.

He began by traveling about the countryside with his Bible, staying with religious families when he was lucky, sleeping outside when he was not. He watched people and listened to their problems, then reflected on what he had seen and heard. He came to know the Scriptures so well, it was said he could have rewritten them had his Bible been destroyed.

After a while, this lonely traveler began to be noticed by the priests, and many attempted to convert
him to their own sects. But Fox sensed a dishonesty in
them. "I went to many a priest to look for comfort," he
wrote, "but found no comfort from them."

Wherever he went, he argued, for George was not
the kind of person to listen passively to anything he
disapproved of. So, he upset some and antagonized
others, for there are not many adults who will listen
patiently and willingly to an outspoken 19-year-old.

Fox even went to London, quite a decision for a
country-bred boy, where he looked up his Uncle Edward Pickering, a Baptist merchant. But neither his
uncle, who George had thought would be an earnest
seeker after spiritual truths, nor the great London professors had any answers for him.

Sadly, George returned to Fenny Drayton in 1644.
There, between his parents who wanted to marry him
off and relatives who thought the army would make a
man of him, he found no peace. "I was grieved," he
said, "that they preferred such things to me." His relatives and neighbors were never to fully understand
him. (Indeed, in the years ahead, when Fox's followers
were counted in the thousands, none of his family or
close relatives—and few if any Drayton folk—accepted
Quakerism.)

Still, this return, unhappy as it was, was in some
ways the start of the Quaker movement, for upon his
return Fox discovered a number of people he termed
"tender." By that he meant a person who was reli-

giously inclined, serious, and earnestly searching for
spiritual truth. The majority of these people were
loosely connected with a sect called Seekers, people
who believed that the Word of God was open and
available to all.

While Fox found some of the people tender, he certainly found no priests that way. One, Nathaniel Stephens, the priest at St. Michael's in Drayton, an old
family friend, spent a good deal of time questioning
George. Stephens had been one of those who had first
tried to push George into the established clergy. He
had even commented about George to the squire of
Fenny Drayton that never "has such a plant been bred
in England." He knew that George had a singular
mind and a thirst for spiritual knowledge, even as a
child, and used him in a strange way. Whatever he
and George spoke about during the weekdays, Priest
Stephens used in his sermons on Sunday. Fox was
angry at what he considered a kind of religious plagia-
rism.

Other priests were no better. One advised Fox to
"take tobacco and sing psalms," advice that might
have soothed a love-sick youth but hardly a God-sick
one. A second suggested a physic and even tried blood-
letting. A third, the learned Dr. Cradock of Coventry,
held a long discussion with George but turned livid
with rage when Fox, by accident, stepped on his flower
bed in the course of their talk. Was it any wonder that
George found such men to be, as he called them,
empty, hollow casks?

Three years of wandering in the fields and orchards, in the countryside and towns, even in the big cities, brought Fox no happiness. He kept going to the priests, those who were supposed to possess the truth, and he found them possessed of nothing but themselves.

Then one morning in 1646, Fox had another vision. In it he heard a voice that told him "All Christians are believers, both Protestants and Papists." This was not an easy idea for a seventeenth century boy to handle. Following that, as he was walking in a field on a Sunday morning, George had a second vision, a corollary of the first, that "to be bred at Oxford or Cambridge was not enough to make a man fit to be a minister of Christ."

Close on those two visions came a third, that "God who made the world did not dwell in temples made with hands . . . but in people's hearts."

Think about those three visions. George Fox was born into a world in which religion played a major, even overpowering role. The important battle of the preceding century had been between Catholics and Protestants as to which owned the Christian truth. Yet Fox was saying both did.

The clergy nurtured its ever-growing authority and claimed that educated priests were the most important interpreters of the truth. Yet Fox was saying education was not what made a man a fit minister.

The churches—both Catholic and Protestant—had money, time, and dogma invested in church buildings.

Yet Fox said God did not dwell in any man-made places at all but in every man's heart.

Those three visions and his response to them were the beginning of George Fox's powerful challenge to the Christian world.

When these three visions became not mere facts but principles to George, truths which he could *know*, could experience, Fox began his own ministry. From then on he used the word "know" to mean knowledge of the Lord proceeding directly from the heart. "I knew these things experimentally," he wrote. (It was this note of personal discovery, of truth being directly revealed from within, called mysticism, that was to become the single most important thing that George Fox and the Quakers were to bring to the world. For though there had been individual Christian mystics before, the Quakers would be the first Christian *group* to practice mysticism.)

Fox's ministry was an odd sort at first, consisting of solitary walks, fasting, mournful midnight wanderings, and hours in hollow trees with his Bible. The soulful wanderer was well aware of the picture he made. "I was a man of sorrows in the time of the first workings of the Lord in me."

When George confronted priests, professors, and non-churchgoers, he was direct with them in his own rough way, brooking no compromise with the principles he had already come to "know." With such an uncompromising nature, it is easy to see why none of the men he went to could answer his questions. It was also easy to see that he was beginning to make enemies.

As George noticed the gaps between what people said and what they did, he challenged them for it. Instead of being humble before age and authority, he treated everyone alike. These thoughts and actions were considered extreme in the seventeenth century, as indeed they are today. Many of the men in power—both religious and civil—would soon come to resent Fox's attacks. Later critics would call Fox intolerant, and indeed he was intolerant of those who did not live as righteously as he did. However, he never asked more of others than he asked of himself.

George Fox began his quest by going to men for answers to his questions. But when all his hope in men was gone, Fox wrote: "then, oh, then, I heard a voice which said 'There is one, even Christ Jesus, that can speak to thy condition'; and when I heard it, my heart did leap for joy."

For George Fox, the lonely seeker, the answer had come "experimentally." It was an answer that would comfort him in times of despair and in his many dark hours in prison. It was the one answer that he would never question—that Christ could speak to a man in his own heart. It was the answer from which all else in his life would follow.

I was sent to turn people from
darkness to light.
    —GEORGE FOX, *Journal*

Chapter 3

The First Ministry

George Fox's early ministry took place in and around
Leicestershire. Though the physical scope of his first
years of preaching was limited to towns he already
knew well, Fox was already sure of the universality of
his message. He felt he was "sent to turn people from
darkness to light." George did not mean that he
wanted to turn them to another new sect. He just
wanted to bring men to what he believed was an honest worship of God, and to proceed directly from that
worship to doing only what was right and good. Fox
wanted to return to the primitive Christianity and
community of the Bible.

George had already been traveling a year when he

met and converted Elizabeth Hooton to his cause. One
of his first fervent followers, Mrs. Hooton was a strong-
willed woman of forty-four with four teen-age children
who had been a Seeker. She was one of those who was
struck immediately by Fox's powerful, rustic preaching. His sincerity had shown through his rough, uneducated words.

Elizabeth Hooton was typical of the thousands who
would soon follow Fox—a Seeker, of the lower class,
willing to give up the easy safe life to follow a precari-
ous calling. She first heard Fox speaking in the house
of Friends, as George termed those people he convinced. The name probably came from the Biblical injunction: "Henceforth I call you not servants, for the
servant knoweth not what his lord doeth; but I have
called you friends." (John 15:15)

Most of Fox's preaching took place in odd places—
in houses, in marketplaces, at fairs, in orchards, in
graveyards, in meadows. George did not like to preach
when asked "to pray at man's will," as he called it. He
spoke only when moved by God. Besides, Fox did not
approve of churches, which he called "steeple-houses."
To him, a man-built church was no holier than any
other building. He liked to say, "The church is the
people . . . and not the house."

Four incidents in those early years of Fox's ministry
show Fox at his best: fervent, outspoken, and ready at
all times to speak his truth to power without counting
the cost.

At one great meeting of professors in Mansfield,

George was sitting quietly listening to an involved
theological discussion. The local priests were arguing
about the blood of Christ, and the professors were listening with great care to the intricate discourse. In
those days theological debating was a common pas-
time.

Suddenly young George jumped up with a cry. "Do
ye not see the blood of Christ? See it in your hearts, to
sprinkle your hearts and consciences from dead works
to serve the living God?"

His outburst so startled the priests and their audience that they tried to shout George down. None of
them had understood what George had been saying
except Captain Amos Stoddard who had arrived late.
He was a man of some authority, and he called out,
"Let the youth speak."

What Fox had been saying was simply this: the
priests were so busy talking *about* the blood of Christ
that none of them understood it was within each and
every one of them. The blood, or the Holy Spirit, was
indwelling, Fox said. He called it the "Inner Light,"
the "Light within," or the "Seed of God."

By this George did not mean reason or conscience,
but something more. An intimate revelation, an en-
lightenment. He based his belief of this "Inner Light"
on what later became known as the "Quaker text" in
the Bible: "That was the true light that lighteth every
man that cometh into the world." (John 1:9)

When George spoke of "dead works" he was not
denying the authenticity of the Bible, but was appeal-

ing instead to the Spirit which originally produced Scripture. To the Puritan priests, the Bible was the final authority, and the Spirit which produced it was no longer in the world. Fox, on the contrary, said that Spirit was not only still in the world, but *in every man.*

This interpretation—or really re-interpretation— was characteristic of the way George Fox saw things. He passed beyond the intricate theology and the theorizing and demanded, in Rufus Jones's words, *"life results."*

Going through the fields on his way to Leicester some time later, young Fox heard about another great meeting in a church in which Presbyterians, Baptists, and Church of England worshipers were going to debate—a theological free-for-all. It was open to anyone and nothing could have stopped George from attending. He said simply, "I was moved by the Lord God to go."

Although the priest was in the pulpit, there was shouting and discussing going on in all directions when George arrived. Men called out questions from the pews and were answered in kind.

Timidly, a woman stood up and asked a question about the birth mentioned in the Bible passage "born again of incorruptible seed, by the Word of God, that liveth and abideth forever." In other circumstances the priests and professors would have spent hours arguing over the meaning of each word.

But the priest was one of those men who, as Fox

aptly put it, "held women have no souls . . . no more
than a goose." He thundered down at the hapless lady,
"I permit not a woman to speak in church."

George, who believed that all people were equal,
stood up and bellowed back at the priest, "Dost thou
call this place a church?"

The priest opened his mouth to speak, but Fox continued uninterrupted. "Or dost thou call this mixed
multitude a church?"

The priest was too old a hand at theological sparring
to be caught that way. He turned the question back on
George. "What do *you* consider a church?"

It was a mistake that the priest would have cause to
regret later. For that question was all the opening
George needed. He began to preach. He said that a
church was "made up of living stones, living members,
a spiritual household, which Christ is the head of; but
He was not the head of a mixed multitude, or of an old
house made up of lime, stones, and wood."

Fox said much, much more. Finally, in desperation,
unable to break in once George had started his compelling oration, the priest and several of his followers
left for a nearby inn. Fox followed them there and pursued the argument. He talked so long and so tirelessly
that he finally talked them down. He recounted somewhat gleefully that "they all gave out and fled away."

This incident, like the Mansfield meeting, was characteristic of Fox. It showed how strongly he felt that all
people were equal. It was also indicative of his feeling
that one must not be silent in the presence of wrong-

thinking or evil. His own spiritual certainty lent Fox the physical strength to verbally browbeat a score of learned priests and theologians.

Fox's physical strength to outpreach and outlast his opponents was to become a byword in England in the next years. In fact one timid Leicestershire priest, hearing George was in his neighborhood, reputedly hid under a hedge until he was gone.

It was during these first few years of his ministry that Fox's concern with social problems was evidenced. He was not only outspoken when it came to matters of the soul, but he found that concern for the soul led directly to matters of the body as well. In modern terms, George Fox was a social activist.

While traveling in Mansfield one fine fall day, George heard that the hiring fair was going on. Men looking for work would stand in line holding some symbol of their skills—a cowherd with a bit of cow tail, a carpenter with a hammer, and the like. The local justices set the wage scale, and anyone convicted of giving *more* than the maximum would go to jail. In that way no man could entice another's worker away.

George decided to preach to the justices setting the wage scale. He missed them at the Bowl-in-Hand Inn where they had been meeting, and heard they had moved on to another town eight miles away. Fox was so fired up about the injustice of the low wages, he ran all the way. He arrived at the town breathless but enthusiastic and exhorted the judges not to be mean in setting the scale of payment. The judges listened to him, and also approved of the fact that he lectured the servants as well.

It was the first experience George had with local magistrates and it was the start of his preaching in courts around the country. He also began to formulate his stand against oath-taking—swearing on the Bible that what was to be said was the truth. It was a stand that would cause Fox and his followers much pain. To George, a man's word—his "yea and nay"—should have been sufficient in any argument, even in a court of law. To take an oath, he argued, was not only a misuse of God's name, but implied a double standard as well. It implied that he would tell the truth only under oath, and would lie at all other times.

Whenever George Fox spoke, whether in steeple-houses or courts of law, in orchard and meadow meetings or in the homes of Friends, he spoke with authority. Did he never question his role or his message? If he had any serious doubts, they were certainly resolved when he was walking through the fields one day in 1649. He felt that God spoke to him saying, "Thy name is written in the Lamb's book of life, which was before the foundation of the world."

This kind of certainty would lead his followers to characterize him as strong-willed and tenacious, his detractors to call him obstinate, intolerant, and opinionated. But it was surely this certainty that lent him the strength to speak out against the powerful priests, even in the very churches where they held sway. For again and again, George Fox challenged the validity of the church to rule, and the authority of Scripture over man's inner promptings. These notions were considered heretical and blasphemous by the English Protestants, and in the seventeenth century, heresy and blasphemy led directly to jail or even to the stake.

Still George Fox spoke out.

In Nottingham, going to a religious meeting with Friends, George spied the spire of St. Mary's Church. Rather than stay with his followers, Fox felt compelled by God to march into the church. There he saw the priest, Nicholas Folkingham, who seemed to him "like a great lump of earth" in his pulpit. Folkingham was preaching the Puritan doctrine that Scripture was the final authority in all arguments.

Now it was the custom in England then that once the priest had finished speaking, anyone might stand up and disagree with him. But George was so moved by what he considered the falsest of doctrines that he "could not hold but was made to cry out and say 'Oh no, it is not the Scriptures.' " He did not wait his turn, nor would he give anyone else a turn to speak. Once he had started, almost no power could stop Fox.

George said that the final authority was the Holy Spirit, the Inner Light within each man. As he continued, the one power on earth that could put, at least temporarily, an end to his argument, arrived. The sheriff's men came into the church. They took Fox by the arm and led him away.

Fox was put into what he termed "a nasty, stinking prison where the wind brought all the stench of the house of office into the place, the stench whereof got so into my nose and throat that it very much annoyed me."

It was his first experience in jail. It would not be his last.

Thou art not to dispute of God,
but to obey him.
 —GEORGE FOX, *Journal*

Chapter 4

A Year in Derby Jail

George Fox's first experience in jail was not a typical
one. John Reckless, the sheriff, was an extremely religious man who was very impressed by the young
preacher. He brought Fox out of prison that same
night and lodged him in his own home. There Mrs.
Reckless met George in the hall and took his hand,
saying, "Salvation is come to our house."

Although he was supposed to be in jail, George remained in the sheriff's house. He even held religious
meetings there. Reckless became such a convinced
Friend that one day, when he was talking with Fox in
his chamber, bedroom slippers on his feet, he suddenly
exclaimed, "I must go into the market and preach re-

pentence to the people." Out went Sheriff John Reckless, slippers and all.

News of Fox's unconventional jail term soon reached
the ears of the magistrate in charge. Fox was summa-
rily popped back into the prison where he remained
for some time. But jail did not make George change his
mind about his ministry. If anything, it hardened his
commitment to God and to the Inner Light.

One day in 1649, while walking in the town of
Mansfield–Woodhouse on a Sunday (or "First Day" as
he called it), Fox felt called to preach "truth to the
priest and people" in their church. He had scarcely
begun when the people, encouraged by their priest, fell
upon George and tried to choke off his words. When
that did not work, the congregation beat him with
their fists and sticks and even their Bibles until he collapsed. Then they hauled him out of the church and
onto the town common where the stocks for criminals
were set up. For hours, his feet and hands bound in the
wooden frame like a common felon, George endured
the jeers of the crowd. Town bullies brought whips and
threatened him. Children threw stones which he could
not dodge. But at last evening came. The pious towns-
people, wearied of their Sunday sport, wandered home
for dinner and George was finally brought before the
local magistrates.

The judges wanted to punish Fox for his terrible
crime: that of preaching that God was within every
person. However, seeing that he had already been
dealt with quite severely, they set him free. This judg-

ment did not please the church folk. They stoned George out of town, threatening him with pistols if he ever returned. He collapsed a mile out of town where some "tenderer" people took him in and cared for him.

All in all, an extraordinary amount of violence had greeted him. But it was not an unusual incident. In his years of traveling and preaching, Fox was to come upon violence again and again. And he was not alone. Almost all the early Friends were beaten, tortured, imprisoned, even killed for saying what they considered to be the truth.

There was something so disturbing about the Friends' truth that many listeners were enraged. That truth so threatened secure lives, so upset ordinary thinking, that many men and women did not dare allow it even to be spoken. And the Friends' answer, George Fox's answer, was always the same—the turned cheek. As William Penn wrote, "He was no more to be moved to fear than to wrath."

One day in Derby, home of the famous Derby fair, the church bells rang out. Fox found out that the bells were signaling a great lecture that was to include priests, army officers, and even a preaching colonel. Of course George went, too.

This time when he stood up to preach to the assembly, he was not mobbed by the congregation. But just after noon, a police officer came and took Fox and his companion away.

The local magistrates were well prepared for

George. It was obvious that they had heard of him and
had been waiting for this opportunity a long time.
They interrogated him until nine o'clock that night.
But even though they had looked forward to this
chance to question Fox, the justices seemed agitated by
his presence. They hurried him out of the room after
each answer so that they might confer about his statements.

Why was there such a fuss made about a simple
country preacher? First of all, the simple country
preacher was beginning to make a name for himself.
To the church powers-that-be, Fox was a left-wing
usurper. They thought that he was bringing in anarchy: if each person could choose how and where and
what to believe in, there would be no church structure
left.

Secondly, Fox was threatening the economic base of
the established church. If there were no churches, and
no priests, there would be little reason or way to tithe
the congregation. The priests were paid by the number
of members in their fold. There were few priests who
would, willingly, give up their jobs when they were
offered no other wages in return.

Finally, the people firmly believed that what George
was saying was blasphemy. Under a law passed in
1648, blasphemy was punishable by death. Though
blasphemy was ill-defined, it was an offense to say that
Scripture was not the word of God or that the dead
would not rise on Judgement Day, or that baptism
(which George belittlingly called "sprinkling") was not

commanded by God. And it was the worst offense of all to call oneself God or Christ.

The interrogation in Derby ran on and on. The judges tried to break the young preacher with words. He cut across their verbiage with the injunction *"Thou art not to dispute of God, but to obey him."* No single sentence of Fox's better sums up his entire theology: by a man's deeds shall you know him.

Yet still the questioning continued:

JUDGES: Are you sanctified? [This was probably the most important question the judges framed. They wanted Fox to admit that he was Christ or that he had the powers of God.]

  Fox: Yes, for I am in the paradise of God.

JUDGES: Have you no sin?

  Fox: Christ my saviour has taken away my sin.

JUDGES: Are you then Christ?

  Fox: Nay; we are nothing, Christ is all.

Try as they might, the judges could not make Fox say that he was God, only that there was God in every man. Still, the judges felt they had heard enough blasphemies to put George in jail for six months.

If they thought jailing would silence him, they were wrong. From prison he began writing many of the letters for which he is justly famous: letters to magistrates, priests, to the Derby mayor, to "the ringers of bells in steeple-houses," and to the growing numbers of Friends, calling each of them to obedience to the Light Within.

Fox had many visitors in jail. Most of them were professors who came to try and make him recant. Fox called them pleaders of "sin and imperfection," for they believed man was born evil while Fox felt man was born with the capacity for good. Fox also felt it was his responsibility to look for, seek out, and call to the good in everyone he met. And this became the ongoing responsibility of each Friend.

The jailkeeper, Thomas Sharman, was one of Fox's chief persecutors at that time. A high professor, he was so enraged by Fox's beliefs that he kept giving bad accounts of George's behavior to the magistrates. One day, though, George overheard Sharman speaking to his wife. The man was greatly troubled and said, "I have seen the day of judgement, and I saw George there; and I was afraid of him because I had done him so much wrong, and spoken so much against him to the ministers and professors and to the justices, and in taverns and alehouses."

Later that night the keeper came into Fox's cell. He sat down beside George on the straw pallet and said, "I have been a lion against you; but now I come like a lamb, and like the jailer that came to Paul and Silas trembling." He asked to stay and talk with George.

Fox replied, "I am in thy power. Thou may do with me as thou will."

Sharman shook his head. "I would have your leave. I wish to be with you always, but not to have you as a prisoner. I have been plagued, my house has been plagued for your sake."

Fox let the man stay and unburden himself. Twelve years later, this same Thomas Sharman would himself be a prisoner for his religious convictions, and write Fox a letter in which he stated: "O happy George Fox! that first breathed that breath of life [to me] within the walls of my habitation!"

In the morning, the keeper left and went to the judges to tell them all that had taken place. One of the judges, Justice Gervase Bennett (whom Fox credited with creating the term "Quaker" because the Friends trembled and quaked at the word of the Lord*) replied that the judges had also been plagued.

Because they wanted to get rid of Fox, the judges agreed to a scheme that would give George a chance to escape. They gave him leave to walk a mile. They assumed he would take the opportunity to run off. But Fox, who understood what they were doing, replied simply that they must show him how far a mile was. He would go that far—and no farther. Foiled, the judges tried a new scheme. They said they would be willing to have George's relatives post bond for his release, that is, buy him out of jail. George refused.

Why was Fox so stubborn? Certainly he would have liked to be free, but not in any way that would compromise his principles. George considered himself innocent of any wrongdoing. To escape, or to pay for his re-

---

* Actually, the term was already in use for other overecstatic sects who quaked, shivered, and trembled in religious fervor. At first the name was used in a derogatory sense, but soon came to have no shame attached to it. William Penn even wrote a pamphlet, "Quakerism, a New Nickname for Old Christianity." Today it is used interchangeably with Friends.

lease, would be agreeing with the reasons for which he
was jailed.

George tried to explain this to Justice Bennett. It so
enraged the judge that he jumped up and ran at Fox,
who was kneeling in prayer. Bennett struck the kneeling Fox about the head and shoulders, and shouted,
"Away with him, jailer, take him away." Fox was
brought back to prison where he finished out his term.

Still, the judges had given George permission to
walk a mile. He proceeded to make use of his mile-
freedom. During the walks, he preached to anyone he
met, so that even while in prison, he continued to
make converts.

In this way, George's six months in the house of correction for blasphemy passed. His term up, he was
about to be released from jail when the conscripters
came to the prison trying to draft men for the Commonwealth army. (The Commonwealth army, under
Oliver Cromwell, was made up of Protestants and
commonfolk fighting against King Charles and his
Catholic wife, Henrietta Maria. This ragtag army was
to finally win its war, behead the king, and found the
British Commonwealth. Oliver Cromwell would soon
become Lord Protector of England.)

Fox was asked to join the army. He was even offered
a captaincy by the soldiers who respected his air of authority and his rough, outspoken ways. Typically,
George did not answer tactfully but spoke his mind.
He said he would never accept a post in the army, for
he was against armies and fighting and war. "I know
where all wars arose, even from the lusts. . . . I live in

the virtue of that life and power that takes away the *occasion* of all wars."

The soldiers were angered by his blunt refusal and instead of shouting for Fox, they changed their cry and began to call, "Take him away, jailer, and put him into the prison amongst the rogues and felons."

Because he had refused to be drafted into Cromwell's army or to fight any kind of war—in fact rejected war as a solution—Fox was put back into jail. This time he was not kept in the house of correction which was a fairly pleasant, open jail. He was thrown instead into a room with thirty felons. He did not even have a bed. This imprisonment lasted six months more.

While he was in jail this time, George began his attack on the jail system, the first in a long line of Quaker prison reform tracts. He wrote to the judges: "What a sore thing it [is] that prisoners should be so long in jail [before their trials] . . . they learn . . . badness one of another in talking of their bad deeds; and therefore speedy justice should be done." It is the same criticism modern reformers make of jails today.

Fox was in Derby prison—first in the house of correction and then in the common jail—for just short of a year. He was released during the harsh winter of 1651, when he was twenty-seven years old. All the while he was in, the common people as well as the judges argued about his "crime" and punishment. He was alternately called a deceiver, seducer, and blasphemer, or an honest, saintly, virtuous man. It was an argument that was to surround him his entire life.

Here are my leather breeches which
frighten all the priests and professors.
                —GEORGE FOX, *Journal*

Chapter 5

The Man in Leather Breeches

The enforced idleness of jail on someone as active as
George Fox had been the worst part of the year-long
imprisonment. He was an unusually restless man, used
to traveling constantly. Indeed, prison was to be the
only place he would remain for any length of time. He
would have eight such rests in his life, for a total of six
years.

Free at last from Derby jail, Fox went out into
Leicestershire through the snow with a joyous reaffir-
mation of faith. Religious meeting followed religious
meeting, and many new Friends were won along the
way.

In 1651, traveling with companions, George had one

of those impulses that frequently came to him. He felt
called by God to leave his friends for the moment and
make his way into the nearby town of Lichfield.

His friends were not so easily left. Because they were
attuned to his moods and afraid that George might
land in jail again so soon after his year in prison, they
were doubly watchful. To escape them, Fox waited
until they had gone into a house. He hung back to be
the last inside, then ducked under a hedge, sneaked
across several ditches, and tracked quickly through the
snow-filled fields. By the time his companions missed
him, George was far away.

He came to a field where a number of shepherds
were standing together, as much for warmth as company. Their sheep nuzzled aside the new snow, searching for grass. It was a familiar scene to George, and he
remembered his years of apprenticeship with George
Gee.

Fox walked over to the shepherds. He felt so fired
with the word of God, he pulled off his shoes and stood
barefoot in the snow. Leaving his shoes with the shepherds, he strode off towards Lichfield.

It was not far to the city. When Fox got there he saw
it was market day. The streets were crowded with
shoppers. George wandered up and down the streets,
and in the marketplace itself, calling at the top of his
voice, "Woe to the bloody city of Lichfield. Woe to the
bloody city of Lichfield."

As George shouted these words, it seemed to him
that there was a ditch of blood in the streets and that

the market was a gigantic pool of blood. Rather than frighten him, though, the vision made him call out the louder: "Woe to the bloody city of Lichfield. Woe to the bloody city of Lichfield."

At last, his message echoing in every street of the city, Fox felt the fervor leave him. He walked out of Lichfield, his feet still on fire with the power of the Lord, across the snowy fields to the same shepherds. There he paid the shepherds for keeping his shoes, found an icy stream in which to wash his feet, and then put his shoes back on.

All this time, not one person had said a word to him.

Why wasn't there a bigger stir at Fox's odd ministry? Why wasn't he hooted at, jeered at, or even put away for his peculiar actions? The reason is that as long as he broke no laws or preached no blasphemy, Fox was free to wander about crying "Woe" as much as he pleased. People of the seventeenth century were used to such oddities. There were too many self-proclaimed prophets and messiahs around those days for one more barefoot minister to make much difference. England had seen the likes of the Ranters who worshiped in loud, jubilant free-for-alls; the Adamites who paraded around nude; and the Diggers who had dug up and planted a commons ten miles from London on which to grow food for the poor. One barefoot prophet walking in the snow did not stir the imaginations of the complacent Lichfield marketers.

Yet George Fox was different, different from the leaders of the Ranters or the Adamites or the Diggers

or the 173 other Independent sects in England. And
his differences were becoming more noticeable every
day.

Physically Fox was outstanding. He was a big-
boned, powerfully-built country boy. He wore his hair
shoulder-length, parted in the middle, contrary to the
Puritan custom of short-cropped hair on men. His
eyes, according to contemporary accounts, were most
extraordinary. They seemed to stare right through a
person and find his soul. People were continually
crying out: "Do not pierce me with thy eyes; keep thy
eyes off me." He had a long nose, but a small mouth,
to judge by the one portrait we have of him, which is of
doubtful authenticity.

His clothes also distinguished him. He was known as
"the man in leathern breeches" because he wore a suit
of leather with "alchemy buttons," buttons of composition metal. He wore leather for practicality rather
than show, since the leather stood up well on his inces-
sant travels.

The leather breeches became associated with Fox.
In fact, once when Fox was at a meeting, he was challenged by an army captain who snidely asked where
Fox's leather suit was. Fox stood up, opened his coat,
and cried: "Here are my leather breeches which
frighten all the priests and professors."

Fox also wore a hat all the time. It was not an affec-
tation, but rather a matter of principle. In the seventeenth century, a man removed his hat in the presence
of authority, nobility, or wealth. It was a sign of sub-

mission to these higher powers. But George believed all people were equal, and not some more equal than others. He would not give "hat honour," as he called it, to any man. Rather, he believed "Honouring all men is reaching that of God in every man."

A crude but powerful speaker with a fine voice, Fox still had the speech patterns of his uneducated youth. It was, as his friend William Penn admitted, "uncouth and unfashionable to nice ears." He had a country accent, his grammar was unpredictable, and he often spoke with metaphors drawn from his farm background. However, Penn went on to say, brokenly as those sentences fell from Fox's lips, they were "often as texts to many fairer declarations."

It is hard for us today to understand how compelling Fox must have been, but a sample of one of his speeches read aloud can serve as a faint echo of his forcefulness. The rhythmic power of this speech, the vigor and urgency of its message, are as moving today as when he first spoke it:

> Sound, sound abroad, you faithful servants of the Lord and witnesses in His name . . . and prophets of the Highest, and angels of the Lord! Sound ye all abroad in the world, to the awakening and raising of the dead, that they may be awakened, and raised up out of the grave, to hear the voice that is living. For the dead have long heard the dead, and the blind have long wandered among the blind, and the deaf amongst the deaf. Therefore sound, sound ye serv-

ants and prophets and angels of the Lord, ye trumpets of the Lord, that ye may awaken the dead, and
awaken them that be asleep in their graves of sin,
death, and hell, and sepulchres and sea and earth,
and who lie in the tombs. Sound, sound abroad, ye
trumpets, and raise up the dead, that the dead may
hear the voice of the Son of God, the voice of the second Adam that never fell; the voice of the Light,
and the voice of the Life; the voice of the Power, and
the voice of the Truth; the voice of the Righteous,
and the voice of the Just. Sound, sound the pleasant
and melodious sound; sound, sound ye the trumpets,
the melodious sound abroad, that all the deaf ears
may be opened to hear the pleasant sound of the
trumpet to judgement and Life, to condemnation
and Light.

In his everyday speech Fox said "thee" and "thou"
to all people, not as was customary only to relatives or
servants, or inferiors. The upper class of the time was
supposed to be addressed with the more formal "you."
George's use of "thee" and "thou," later called "plain
language," was a matter of principle, as was his refusal
to give hat honour.

Just as his speaking was often littered with ungram-
matical statements, so was his writing. Though George
knew the Bible in minute detail, his writing was never
as smooth as his example. He was never able to write
without crude mistakes in grammar. Even his *Journal,* a
close account of his calling and ministry, was vastly ti-

died up by a succession of loving secretaries and editors.

Finally, George's strength and ability to endure
physical hardship was well known. He lasted through
long and difficult imprisonments. He slept little. He
ate sparingly. He traveled wet, cold, and hungry. He
suffered the attacks of hostile crowds with a patience
and calmness that won hundreds to his cause. It was
even rumored that he never slept at all. A Patrington
man invited George home that bleak winter of 1651,
and watched while George climbed into bed just to be
sure that such a thing actually happened.

Charges of magic and wizardry followed Fox wherever he went because of his ability to endure so much
and to avoid the many snares his enemies set for him.
Fox was rumored to ride a devilish black horse that
could be in two places at once. It was said that he carried a bottle of magic potion that bewitched people
into following him.

It was far easier for people to believe that Fox had
magic potions to make people love him than to realize
that his charismatic personality could make him such
a powerful leader. Yet over and over, that overwhelm-
ing personality was attested to. A doctor in Lancaster,
so full of hatred that he declared he would run Fox
through with a rapier even though he be hanged for it
immediately, became a loving Friend after hearing
Fox speak. An Ulverstone priest hurried out of his
church when Fox spoke there, for he feared the trembling church would fall down around his ears.

Other people may have feared witchcraft in Fox's ability to capture the hearts of his listeners, but Fox himself knew that it was because he spoke with the absolute certainty of his message. As he put it himself: "If but one man were raised by [God's] power to stand and live in the same Spirit that the prophets and apostles [did] that man should shake all the country. . . ."

Shake the country he did. The first really large shakings occurred in Yorkshire in 1652. Until that time, Fox had won people over singly or in small groups. But in 1652 he visited the North country. In Yorkshire there were great communities of Seekers, the sect which consisted of people who wanted to bring the church back to its original purity. They did not think of themselves as a separate church, but rather as an interim congregation waiting for the proper time to reestablish the true church. The Seekers sat in their meetings in silence waiting for God to speak to them. Unless a person felt moved by the Spirit of the Lord to speak out, he remained silent. Because of this, the Seekers were also called "Waiters." They were not only awaiting the word of God; they were also waiting for a new prophet to come and lead them.

It was to this mystical, deeply religious community in Yorkshire that George Fox came.

Pendle Hill, a fairly steep hill in Lancashire, has a commanding view of the Irish Sea. When Fox traveled towards Yorkshire in 1652, he felt moved to labor up the hill. There on top of Pendle Hill, he had a vision of

"a great people to be gathered." The Yorkshire Seekers? George believed so. He scrambled down the hill
ecstatic, pausing only to drink at a clear spring, which
is still called "George Fox's well."

That same night, Fox came to a country inn. While
there he had another vision of the great people, this
time all clad in white raiment by a river. The river of
that vision he identified as the Rawthey which flowed
through the Yorkshire hills where one of the largest
Seeker communities lived.

Quite soon after George's two visions, the Seekers
gathered for their regular General Monthly Meeting
at Preston-Patrick. Two of their foremost ministers,
Francis Howgill and John Audland, spoke convincingly at the early morning chapel. Both Howgill and
Audland were dedicated young preachers. George listened in at the door of the chapel, but did not come
inside. He was pleased with the size of the gathering—over 1,000 people—and their general attentive-
ness. He was also impressed by the sincerity of their
preachers and the fact that Howgill, a tailor, and Audland, a textile merchant, were not paid for their services.

When the meeting broke up, Fox invited the Seekers
and their ministers to an outdoor meeting to be held
after lunch.

George's reputation for powerful preaching had
most probably preceded him. Howgill and Audland
and many of their followers showed up in the afternoon. They sat on the grass before a large outcropping

of rocks. From this natural rock pulpit, George prepared to preach to them. But he did not start as soon as the crowd quieted down. Instead, he stood for many minutes in silence, waiting for God's presence. When he finally felt moved to speak, Fox preached for more than three hours. He talked about the holiness of places, of God being within each man, and how God had called him to preach. Finally, he told the gathered people that they should no longer be Seekers and Waiters but could now be Finders, possessors of God's truth.

For many of the people there that day, there was no doubt—George Fox was the prophet for whom they had been waiting. The entire outdoor meeting was such a moving experience that many hundreds of Seekers became "Children of the Light," as Fox's followers were soon called. (This was probably because of the Biblical phrases: "walk as children of light" [Eph. 5:8] and "ye are all the children of light" [I Thess. 5:5].) Howgill, who was slightly older than Fox, and Audland, who was a little younger, became not only followers but also his close associates from then on.

It was truly a time of shaking the country. George Fox had indeed gathered "a great people," the first large-scale conversion to the Quaker way. Equally as important, he was beginning to gather around him a band of preachers who, in Rufus Jones's words were "only slightly less gifted than himself": Howgill, Audland, Richard Farnsworth, Edward Burrough, John Camm, and the unfortunate James Nayler.

. . . and if all England had been there,
I thought they could not have denied
the truth of those things.
—Margaret Fell

Chapter 6

Meeting the Fells

Swarthmore Hall was undeniably the largest house in
Ulverston. While other houses in the area had no more
than five fireplaces counted in the hearth tax, Swarthmore Hall had thirteen. It was the home of Thomas
Fell, one of the leading men in northern England, a
member of Parliament and a prominent judge. He
lived at Swarthmore Hall with his wife Margaret and
their eight children.

Margaret Askew Fell, a wealthy woman in her own
right, was only eighteen when she married the 34-year-
old Fell, but she was already an educated, well-spoken
young lady. She grew into a thoughtful, religious, gentle but firm-minded wife and mother. She also became

competent in managing the large household during the judge's frequent absences from home on court matters.

Because Mistress Fell was extremely interested in matters of religion, and the judge a liberal gentleman, Swarthmore Hall had become a stopping place for itinerant preachers. All kinds of professors came to the great Elizabethan manor house, and none was turned away.

Yet, as interested as she was in the many new ways of seeing God, Margaret Fell still attended the regular Church of England church in Ulverston, listening intently to the outspoken rector, William Lampitt. Lampitt, an Oxford graduate, was an extremely opinionated man who had a reputation as a gossipmonger. Mistress Fell was not wholly satisfied with her priest. In fact, she had only recently had a strange dream about a man in a white hat coming to Ulverston to confound the priests.

In 1651, not long after Mistress Fell's dream, George Fox came to Ulverston and made his way to Swarthmore Hall. He arrived on a day when both the judge and his wife were away, Fell heading the assizes in Wales and Margaret out for the afternoon. However, priest Lampitt was there. He often visited Swarthmore Hall, for he was both a personal friend of the Fells and a kinsman as well.

Lampitt had certainly heard of Fox, whose reputation had preceded him from Yorkshire. He settled down for a long theological discussion with George. Lampitt was prepared to be friendly with the infamous young preacher, for the priest was always willing to spend a pleasant evening in friendly religious sparring. He was one of those popular psalm-singing preachers to whom the priesthood was an easy way of making a living. Naturally enough, Fox took an immediate dislike to him, writing that Lampitt was "full of filth."

It was inevitable that Fox and Lampitt would end up in a painfully loud and heated argument that ended only when Lampitt stamped away angrily.

The youngest Fell girls—Sarah, Mary, and Susannah—had overheard the argument between their pleasant priest and the tall stranger who would not remove his hat. They were so upset that the minute their mother returned from her outing they told her the whole tale. Margaret was pained that such a fight had occurred in her house, but she was also fascinated by the strange preacher. Was he the white-hatted man about whom she had dreamed? He had certainly confounded Priest Lampitt. Mistress Fell spent the evening with her family and servants, listening to Fox explain his convictions.

The next day Lampitt was back to renew the argument. He and George spent the entire day in disagreement, this time in front of Margaret Fell. Since Lampitt's livelihood depended upon the loyal support of parishioners like the Fells, the Ulverston rector put aside his jolly ways and fought as hard as he could.

But three days later, Fox was still at Swarthmore Hall, undefeated.

Although she was very much impressed with Fox,

Mistress Fell was still not totally convinced. As she prepared to go as usual to Lampitt's church on Sunday, she asked George to go with her. He accompanied her as far as the church but refused to enter, walking instead in a nearby field until he felt God wished him to go in. When he finally felt moved to enter the church, Lampitt was leading the congregation in a hymn. As they finished and sat down, George, uninvited, stood up on a pew and began to preach.

This so incensed John Sawrey, a conservative Puritan and local justice, that he jumped to his feet shouting, "Take him away."

Two officers immediately got up and took George by the arm when Margaret Fell got to her feet. "Let him alone; why may not he speak as well as any other?"

The officers backed away and George continued to preach. As he spoke, Margaret Fell felt his words cut straight to her heart. She sat down in her pew again and cried bitterly. As the tears raced down her cheeks, she thought, "We are all thieves, we are all thieves, we have taken the Scriptures in words and know nothing of them in ourselves."

Many of the congregation were moved as well. Justice Sawrey finally had Fox put out of the church, but George continued to speak in the graveyard. Margaret and half the congregation followed him there.

That evening, the Fell family and servants gathered again in the parlor to listen to Fox. They asked questions when they did not understand an important point, but mostly they listened as George talked about

the Inner Light that was God in each man. They also
spent a long time in silent prayer. When the evening
was done, almost everyone who had been in the parlor
was a convinced Friend.

Fox left Swarthmore Hall for three weeks to preach
in the countryside. While he was gone, Lampitt and
Sawrey did their best to spread rumors about Fox's
wizardry. When they heard that Judge Fell was on his
way home, Lampitt and Sawrey gathered together a
large party of Puritans who hated George (including
overweight Captain Sands to whom Fox had said
rather cruelly, "Thee must have a new god, for thy
god is thy belly"). The group came upon Fell as he was
riding across the Morecambe Sands.

"Your wife and household have been bewitched,"
was their greeting. This was a terrible charge in those
days when men really believed in witchcraft.

Judge Fell hurried home and found his wife and
children strangely subdued. He also found two Quaker
preachers in residence, James Nayler and Richard
Farnsworth. But George, the wizard and blasphemer,
was not due back until evening.

It is fortunate that Judge Fell was a calm, sensible
man who had a great deal of trust and faith in his wife.
He listened with an open mind to Nayler and Farnsworth, both gifted speakers, and he refused to condemn
Fox unheard.

Still it was true that the household seemed bewitched. Dinner was a strange affair. The children
were unnaturally quiet, not even wishing to show off

on their musical instruments for their father who had been away almost a month. And then suddenly Margaret began to quake and tremble at the dinner table. The judge was, in Margaret's words, "struck with amazement." Poor Margaret felt torn, she later admitted, for she feared that "either I must displease my husband or offend God."

At last Fox arrived. The judge consented to see him alone in the parlor. Hat on head, without any of the preliminary bowings and scrapings with which the common folk usually greeted a justice, George began to talk to Fell.

He spoke with the judge for many hours, and as they talked, the entire Fell family and servants crept silently into the room. Nayler and Farnsworth came in, too. Fox spoke "excellently as ever I heard him," said Margaret, ". . . and if all England had been there, I thought they could not have denied the truth of those things."

Certainly Judge Fell did not. Though Lampitt arrived early the next morning, it was too late. As Margaret was to write years later, "My husband had seen so much the night before that the priest got little entrance upon him."

The convincing of Margaret Fell was a large turning point in the early history of the Friends. It was the first time an educated, well-born family had been converted to Quakerism. And though one of the main tenets of the Quaker faith was the equality of all people, it is easier to convince a man of lower standing that he is equal to a high-born man than to convince the high-born man of the same. In fact, George's own social standing often stood in the way of his winning over the well-educated professors. Still, as Penn, a courtier and a nobleman, wrote: Fox was "civil beyond all forms of breeding." It was this civility that Thomas and Margaret Fell saw.

More important than the fact that the Fells were well-born, was the fact that both Judge and Mistress Fell became active friends to the Quakers. The judge turned over Swarthmore Hall to them, and a great Meeting was held there in 1652 and continued regularly until 1690, when a Meeting House was built nearby.

George used to preach from a balcony outside the judge's second-floor bedroom and the judge listened to all the meetings through the open door of his study. The large attic at Swarthmore Hall became a dormitory to accommodate traveling Friends. Swarthmore Hall, in the years to come, was to be both a center from which Quaker evangelists set out and where they returned to rest or recuperate from frequent beatings and jailings. While the judge never actually became a Friend, he had such sympathy for them that he used his influence and authority to protect the Quakers as much as he could.

Most important, though, was the conversion of Margaret Fell. She became the "Mother of Quakerism," and was described by Thomas Camm, one of the Yorkshire Seekers, as "a tender nursing mother unto many, condescending in great humility to those of low degree." Mistress Fell was the force behind Swarthmore Hall as the center of Quaker information. She maintained a regular correspondence with itinerant preachers and Friends in prison. Because of her care in preserving the first letters of the young, growing Quaker movement, some 1,400 priceless documents that relate to the birth of the Friends were saved.

Margaret Fell also became the treasurer of the young Quaker movement, pledging not only her own fortune but finding many other donors as well. And eighteen years after she first met George Fox, ten years after the judge's death, Mistress Fell became George Fox's wife.

The cry was among the people that the Quakers had got the day, and the priests were fallen.

—GEORGE FOX, *Journal*

Chapter 7
The Word Is Spread

Justice Sawrey and his priestly friends, having failed in their first attempts to discredit Fox with the Fells and other North Country supporters, decided to have George imprisoned. The charge they concocted was the old one. Fox, they said, claimed to be divine.

Sawrey and his friends were careful to issue a warrant for Fox's arrest when Judge Fell was out of the district on his court circuit. They knew that the judge's influence was too great for them to have Fox arrested when the judge was around. Unfortunately for them, Fell returned before the warrant could be served, and the officials were so afraid of him, they conveniently lost the papers.

However, everyone—including Judge Fell—reck-
oned without George. When he heard that charges
were being leveled against him, Fox had looked forward to the confrontation. He gloried in debate, for it
was the one chance he had to convince those who
would not otherwise listen to him.

If Fox had a major fault, it was this simple kind of
vanity. Not that he was vain of his own powers, for he
felt he could convince only because his message was directly from God. He often said that, once heard, the
message could not be denied, and he did everything in
his power to let the message be heard, whether people
wanted to listen or not.

When the charges against him were quietly
dropped, George decided to travel to Lancaster to defend himself anyway. He would *insist* on a trial. After
unsuccessfully trying to dissuade him from such a trip,
Judge Fell rode with Fox, to help him in the legal as-
pects of the case.

At the Lancaster courtroom, forty priests vied with
one another to lie about George. However, all their evidence was hearsay and secondhand. None of them
had heard George preach. Besides that, not one of
them even understood what they had gotten secondhand. Fox's presence in the courtroom so upset them
that one after another the priests broke down on the
witness stand.

In the middle of the chaotic hearing, one of the
judges, Colonel William West, suddenly felt himself
miraculously cured of a long-standing illness. He was

positive that George had done it. "George," he said, "if thou hast anything to say to the people, thou mayest freely declare it."

And freely George did.

He spoke about the Bible and about the Spirit of God that was within each man. What he said so enraged the forty priests that they finally found their tongues and began to shout at him. One priest blurted out, "The Spirit and the Scriptures are inseparable." It was a common belief of the day.

But it was not Fox's belief. He replied, "Then every one that hath the letter hath the Spirit; and they might buy the Spirit with the letter of the Scripture." He meant if the two were inseparable, a man might carry the Holy Spirit in his pocket along with his Bible.

Fox's argument so carried the court that the judges were forced to discharge George, much to Sawrey's chagrin.

Under Sawrey's instigation, the forty priests immediately tried to draft an appeal. They even persuaded a friendly justice to issue a warrant. But Colonel West, who was also the court clerk, refused to write it out. When the judge insisted, West told him to write it himself. West added that, rather than see Fox unjustly persecuted, he would forfeit his own estates and go to jail in George's stead. This so impressed the judge that he withdrew his support from the priests and the affair was dropped at last.

"The cry was among the people that the Quakers

had got the day and the priests were fallen," wrote George of the victory. But it was a bitter and costly victory. Fox had made some very powerful enemies and they were soon to find a way to imprison him again.

Fox moved on from Lancaster to Carlisle, but his very presence in the city brought disruption. Even the magistrates' wives, it was said, were ready to run at him and pull out his hair. So the magistrates and justices got together and granted a warrant against him, committing him to prison as a "blasphemer, a heretic, and a seducer."

It was the same offense they had charged George with in Derby. This time there was an added danger. Fox could be hanged as a second-offender of a blasphemy charge under the Act of 1648.

Fox's second imprisonment was not as easy as his first. He was thrown into a filthy cell with thieves and murderers, men and women together, where the inmates were so bug-ridden that, wrote George, "one woman was almost eaten to death with lice." The jailers he described as "bear-herders," who went out of their way to persecute him. They let none of George's friends visit him, yet paraded in great ladies to titter at the famous Quaker who lay in a pest-ridden cell. The jailers also passed through rude priests who ranted at George as late as ten o'clock at night. Furthermore, one of the jailers delighted in cudgeling Quakers "as if he had been beating a pack of wool." His favorite target was George.

One time, when this brutal jailer was belaboring

Fox with a large stick, George unexpectedly burst into song. It so angered the jailer that he beat George harder, but George only kept singing louder. In a rage, the jailer dropped his stick and ran out to a local inn and fetched back a fiddler, hoping to annoy Fox. But George merely raised his voice louder still, finally drowning out both the fiddler and the jailer, and they left in a huff.

One of the justices who had been against Fox heard of the incredible conditions of the jail, and he came to inspect the prison in person. He was so appalled at the filth and stench that great changes were made immediately. The beastly jailer was himself imprisoned for unreasoned cruelty.

This was the kind of ironic twist of fate that seemed to afflict all of George's enemies: jailers being jailed, torturers being tortured. George referred to the people who suffered such retribution as being "cut off by God." It was a kind of arrogance or pride on Fox's part which, along with his vanity, came from his certainty that he possessed God's truth. It is a fault he shared with many of the Old Testament prophets.

The Carlisle magistrates found, after a while, that there was no evidence to support the charges against Fox. They let him go without ever having brought him to trial. He had been in jail seven weeks, eaten by bugs, lying in the filth, beaten by a cruel jailer, while merely awaiting trial.

This second imprisonment of Fox's produced a peculiar phenomenon. Instead of weakening Fox's hold on his movement, which is what the local magistrates had hoped (they worked on an "out of sight, out of mind" policy), Fox's followers grew in great numbers in the North. Fox himself was aware of this phenomenon, and mentioned it in one of his letters. "The more I was cast into outward prisons, the more people came out of their spiritual and inward prison," he wrote.

All the Quaker preachers were beginning to draw huge crowds in their outdoor meetings. They called these large public gatherings "threshing meetings" because in it the speakers attempted to separate the wheat (those who could receive the Quaker truth) from the chaff (those who could not). Howgill and Burrough, two of the early Quaker preachers, wrote about such gatherings to Margaret Fell, saying, "we two were in the general meeting place among the rude world, threshing and plowing."

Priests who had previously prophesied that the Children of the Light would never last six months began to make different predictions. The Quakers, they now said, would "eat one another out." The priests foresaw that the wandering evangelists, who refused to take any payment but were fed and sheltered by Friends, would soon outeat and outstay their welcomes. But it did not happen that way. The Quaker preachers, while not well-fed or well-clothed, still continued to prosper. And the Friends in business, instead of being eaten-out, began to prosper, too.

At first, the Quakers' strange speech and strange

ways had so frightened the people with whom they traded that they were boycotted. But soon they became known as the most honest and trustworthy tradesmen around. Unlike others, the Quakers would never bargain. They set fair prices to begin with and were scrupulously fair in all their dealings. In fact, it was soon said that "If we let these Quakers alone, they will take the trade of the nation out of our hands." So rather than eating Friends out of house and home, the roving Quaker preachers, by spreading the word of Quaker honesty, benefitted other Friends.

At the same time, the preachers in Fox's band had moved out of the small villages and towns and had expanded their activities into such large cities as London and Bristol. There they found so many listeners that, as they wrote, their "net is likely to break with fishes."

Flushed with success, George himself began to move out of the North. He went to join many of his troop of sixty young vigorous preachers in the south of England. It was a remarkable group. They were unfazed by the hardships they encountered and even seemed to welcome persecution. Called "First Publishers of Truth" and "The Valiant Sixty," they were not priests by trade. Some were farmers and craftsmen and businessmen, several were men of education, and twelve were women. A few had even been members of the Swarthmore household, including a steward, a family retainer, and a clerk. All had left their homes to face hard travel, adversity, and even death in God's service. In Penn's words, they were "calling people to repentance and to turn to the Lord with their hearts as well as their mouths."

As Fox and the Publishers traveled south, George stopped at Fenny Drayton. He had not been there for over three years. He gave a truly powerful sermon in the town, besting his old foe, Nathaniel Stephens and seven other priests before hundreds of onlookers.

Fox's father, that "Righteous Christer" Christopher Fox, still a regular churchgoer despite his son's revolutionary activities, attended the meeting. He listened intently to George's words. Then he thwacked his cane on the ground and said, "Well, I see that he that will but stand to the truth, it will carry him out." It was a fitting tribute to his son's ministry.

Now I see there is a people risen
that I cannot win with gifts or
honours, offices or places; but all
other sects and people I can.
—OLIVER CROMWELL

Chapter 8

Meeting Oliver Cromwell

In 1650, the army of common people won the Civil
War. It was a victory for the Puritans who, under the
leadership of Oliver Cromwell, took over the ruling of
England. The Catholic Queen Henrietta Maria and
her sons Charles Stuart and James fled to the Continent, but King Charles I was captured and executed.

It was a tumultuous time in England, but George
Fox and his followers seemed only peripherally involved with the social and political upheavals. However, they were quite aware when Cromwell was made
Lord Protector, for he promised freedom of worship for
all Englishmen.

Though unlike in many ways, Oliver Cromwell and

George Fox were two of a kind. Both were typical products of the religious turmoil of the seventeenth century. Yet both were visionary enough to see farther than the newly-translated Bible. This helped set them apart from other Englishmen of the day. Overpowering personalities, they were vilified by their enemies and worshiped by their followers, who tended to credit them with a saintliness that only lessened their great stature as humans. And both, in their own ways, were trying to free the people of England: Cromwell from the tyranny of the nobles, Fox from the tyranny of the priests.

It was inevitable that the two should meet and respect one another.

In 1653, six months after Oliver Cromwell was made Lord Protector, the Quakers planned a large meeting of Friends in Whetstone where long moments of silence would alternate with preaching, usually by a "public Friend" used to speaking to big gatherings. Afterwards, anyone convinced by the meeting would be sent on to smaller silent meetings in the neighborhood. If there were no local meetings, the "public Friends" would help start one.

The Whetstone Meeting was to be the usual Friends Meeting, but the times were different. The new Puritan government was still uneasy. It had won its position in blood, and so it saw sedition in all large gatherings, heard treason in every unorthodox statement. The government had good cause to worry. The wounds of the Civil War were still open. There were many people unhappy enough to plot to overthrow the republic, though the Quakers were not among them.

Seventeen troopers came to arrest the Whetstone Friends. They were led by Colonel Francis Hacker who had signed Charles I's death sentence and supervised the king's execution.

Colonel Hacker was not anxious to have a confrontation with the Children of the Light, even though his loyalty to Cromwell was beyond question. Both the colonel's wife and his chief adviser were already "tender" towards the Quakers. In later years they both became Friends.

Still, the charge of plotting to overthrow the government was a serious one, even if Hacker doubted the truth of the charge. For that reason, the colonel and his troopers proceeded to Whetstone. When they got there, they found that the "public Friend" preaching at the meeting was none other than George Fox. Hacker was easily persuaded to let all the other Friends go and have Fox answer for them all.

George denied that the Friends were plotting to overthrow anyone. He explained that Quakers were not interested in the political structure of the state and were meeting for religious reasons only.

Colonel Hacker already knew this, but he still tried to persuade the Friends not to hold any more meetings. In a firm yet polite interview with Fox, Hacker said, "You may go home and keep at home, George, if you will not go abroad to any more meetings."

Fox's only answer was "I am an innocent man, free

from plots. . . . If I promise this, it would manifest that I was guilty of something. It would make my home a prison. And if I went to [religious] meetings, thee would say I broke thy order. I *shall* go to meetings as the Lord should order me." And George added, in case his answer appeared in any way treasonable, *"We are a peaceable people."*

The colonel shook his head. "Well, then, I will send you tomorrow morning by six o'clock to my Lord Protector."

Fox was taken away to spend the night in prison under guard. The next morning, at precisely six, one of Cromwell's special lifeguards, Captain Drury, came to collect the prisoner. George asked to speak to Hacker before they left, and was brought immediately to the colonel's bedchamber. Hacker was still in bed.

Sitting up, Colonel Hacker restated his plea. "I can only say *go home*, George, and keep no more meetings."

If Fox had expected to hear anything else, he showed no disappointment. In fact it seemed as if he had asked for the early morning meeting only to reiterate his own views. "I can not submit to that," he replied, "but must have my liberty to serve God."

Hacker shook his head at the prisoner. "Then you must go before the Protector."

At that, Fox knelt by the bedside and prayed loudly to God to forgive Hacker whom he likened to Pilate, washing his hands of the matter. Then he added cryptically, "And when the day of thy misery and trial comes upon thee, I bid thee remember what I said to thee now."

It was a scene that Hacker was to recall vividly a few years later after the death of Cromwell and the Restoration of the Monarchy. Two days before Hacker's own execution, when he was imprisoned in the Tower of London, Margaret Fell visited him. He told her of his last words with Fox and how true the prophecy had been.

The task fell to Captain Drury to escort Fox to London. For Drury, a Quaker-hater, it was a thankless task. All along the way, George stopped to preach to the passers-by, and there was no way Drury could ignore that loud, powerful voice. It was a long journey, broken frequently by Fox's sermons to their fellow travelers. In desperation, Drury told Fox he would let him go if he would only go straight home and hold no more meetings. Drury had no authority to do this, but he didn't care. Fox's answer to Drury was the same as it had been to Hacker.

At last they reached London. Drury lodged Fox at the Mermaid Inn without guard, in the vain hope that the Quaker would run away. But when he returned from seeing the Lord Protector, Fox was still there. What Drury did not understand was that George was delighted to have the opportunity to meet Oliver Cromwell and to preach the Quaker truth to him.

The captain was forced to admit that Cromwell was interested in hearing from Fox. He wanted a letter of promise from George that he would not take up weapons against the young government.

George wrote a letter to Cromwell, but it was not exactly the kind of document the Lord Protector had in
mind. In it, Fox explained that he would not take up
arms against Cromwell *or any other man,* and that he was
sent by God to stand as a witness against *all* violence. It
was a tacit condemnation of Cromwell, for Cromwell
had formed the army that had first divided, then con-
quered England, and sent the king to the executioner.
However, Cromwell was a wise enough man to understand the motives that drove Fox to write that letter,
and he sent for Fox.

George was not the first Quaker with whom Oliver
Cromwell had come in contact. He had already met
two of the Publishers of Truth—Howgill and Camm.
And another Friend, Thomas Aldam, had ripped a
cap to shreds before him in a symbolic act showing
how Cromwell's advisers would be ripped asunder.
The Lord Protector had formed the notion, as many
educated people had, that Quakers were simply fools
or fanatics. (As one bishop later wrote, the Quakers
"had their beginnings from the very rabble and dregs
of people.") However, Cromwell was not close-minded
on the subject, and he was curious to meet Fox.

Drury brought Fox to Whitehall, and they arrived
early in the morning before the Lord Protector was
fully dressed. Fox neither took off his hat nor gave any
more formal greeting than "Peace be in this house" before he began to preach to Cromwell.

Cromwell was not the kind of man to be preached at
or to suffer fools, so he must have been interested in

what George had to say, for Fox talked at length. He was interrupted only when Cromwell nodded agreement and said, "It is good" or "It is truth."

When some people entered who had business with Cromwell, Fox finished speaking and turned to leave.

Cromwell strode over to George and caught him by the hand. With tears in his eyes, the Lord Protector said, "Come again to my house; for if thou and I were but an hour of a day together, we should be nearer one to the other." And then he added, "I wish thee no more ill than I do my own soul."

"If thee does," Fox replied, "thee wrongs thy soul."

On orders from the Lord Protector himself, Captain Drury took Fox down to the great dining hall where Cromwell's men were eating. But George refused to sit, saying, "Tell the Lord Protector that I will not eat of his bread nor drink of his drink."

It was reported later that Cromwell, on hearing this, said, "Now I see there is a people risen that I can not win with gifts of honours, offices or places; but all other sects and people I can."

A novel might end at this point with the words that after meeting with Oliver Cromwell, George Fox and the Quakers were never again troubled. But history does not imitate art, at least not often enough. Certainly Cromwell was moved by Fox and responded immediately to him. But the ruler of a country is moved by many things, not the least of which are international incidents.

Not long after his talk with Fox and bothered by the

continuing plotting by Catholic Jesuits both in and out of the country, Cromwell issued an order that greatly curtailed freedom of worship. Ostensibly the order, called the Oath of Abjuration, required that Catholics —or persons suspected of Catholicism—had to forswear allegiance to the Pope under pain of imprisonment and loss of property.

Like all loyalty oaths, it was worse than useless. Anyone who is truly plotting something is usually willing to swear to anything at all. The ones caught by such an oath are generally the innocents, like the Quakers who are against taking oaths. It is an irony of history that the Quakers were prosecuted under the law as much, or more than, the Catholics for whom it was intended.

Which of you would do as much for me
if I were in the same condition?
—OLIVER CROMWELL

Chapter 9

Doomsdale

The Oath of Abjuration was the single most important
law in early Quaker history. Because of it, many Children of the Light were unjustly imprisoned for long pe-
riods of time—the charge, treason.

Even when their prison terms were up, the Quakers
stayed on in jail, for they refused to pay the fees owed
the wardens. It was the law then that prisoners had to
foot the bill for their stay in jail, and they were to remain in jail until the fees were paid. But the Friends,
feeling that they were imprisoned unjustly and therefore owed nothing, refused to give the jailers any
money. So the Quakers were often imprisoned for
months, even years, past their actual terms.

The most prominent Friend to be jailed in this manner was George Fox himself.

It happened during Fox's preaching tour of the southern counties in 1655. George and Edward Pyot had been riding together near the town of Ives when Pyot's horse threw a shoe. While Pyot rode back into town to have his horse re-shod, Fox strolled down by the seaside for silent, solitary meditation. It was one of the few times in several years he had been alone outside of prison. After a while, George followed Pyot back to town and found it in an uproar. Pyot and another Friend had been dragged into Major Peter Ceely's house for an impromptu hearing.

Fox could not find out from the unruly mob what the charges were beyond the fact that the men were Quakers. So he marched into Ceely's house and dressed the major down for letting the people of Ives get out of hand.

Ceely was startled at first, but when he realized that the irate man before him was George Fox, the chief Quaker himself, Ceely was delighted. Without any work on his own part, Ceely had gotten Fox in his hands. He quickly produced a paper which George had written to seven parishes in the district and asked if Fox would claim it. He expected Fox to hedge or even disclaim any knowledge of the paper which was a blunt warning that those who did not believe properly in Christ would be cut off from God's love and protection. But Ceely obviously did not know his man. Without hesitating, George replied, "Yes."

Immediately, Ceely asked Fox to take the Oath of Abjuration, knowing full well that Fox would refuse. When George obliged him by refusing, Ceely turned his attention to questioning the other two Quakers.

George started to sit down when a local priest ran at him, screaming that his hair was too long. Because of his shoulder-length hair, George was often badgered by perfect strangers. It was the Puritan style to have bowl haircuts (in fact, the nickname for Puritans was "Roundhead") and the Quakers' long hair often enraged otherwise peaceable people.

Fox replied, "I will not cut it, though many are offended at it. I have no pride in it. It is not of my putting on."

Major Ceely took a while deciding that he had enough evidence—because of the oath—to send the Quakers to jail. On a Sunday, he detailed a party of horse soldiers to escort the Friends to jail. The soldiers were well armed, with both pistols and swords.

Fox, however, refused to travel on the Sabbath. Indeed, it was quite unusual for people of the time to travel that day. He began to argue with the soldiers about the blasphemy of traveling on Sunday, and it was not long before a crowd had gathered. Unable to let such an opportunity slip by, Pyot, who was a "public Friend," began to preach to the people. Fox, who had been too busy arguing with the soldiers to notice the crowd, suddenly realized that there was quite an audience and turned his attention to them. Pyot in turn lectured the soldiers.

While the two Friends engaged the attention of all the people outside, the third prisoner sneaked away and strolled over to the local church where services were in progress. There he climbed upon a pew and began to preach to the priest and congregation. This so incensed the people, they leaped upon him and began to beat him.

With a minimum of effort and in a matter of minutes, the three Quakers had seized the attention of almost the entire town of Ives. If they had planned such a maneuver, they probably would not have done half so well. But the preaching Friends were so in tune with one another, and so filled with a desire to spread the word of Quaker truth, that such opportunities continually opened to them.

The noise in the church as the congregation attacked the Quaker preacher alerted the soldiers to the fact that one of their three prisoners had escaped. They raced over to the church to find him. When they saw that the Friend was being beaten by the church folk, they did not rescue him. Instead they turned in a rage on Fox and Pyot, and threatened to kill the two of them for having created such an uproar. George, in a calm voice, managed to soothe the enraged soldiers and they at last got the third Friend away from the angry mob.

However, the events of the morning made the troopers harden their resolve to travel at once, Sunday or not. In the afternoon, the prisoners were set upon horses and led away.

They had scarcely reached the town line when Fox broke away from the soldiers and rode back into Ives. He felt moved, he said, to preach to an old man back in town. The soldiers drew their pistols and ordered him to halt. But George continued riding, trusting God to guard his back (and the soldiers to miss a moving target), and he delivered his sermon to the surprised old man in Ives.

The troopers were understandably provoked by this behavior. They had been made fools of in a way they could not understand. Their weapons had not helped them at all. They were ready to try anything to rid themselves of their captives—even murder.

That evening, the leader of the soldiers, Captain John Keate, sent several of his soldiers to kill the Quakers in their beds. But Pyot had had a premonition, and uncharacteristically, the Quakers had locked their door.

The next day, Keate tried again. This time he let his demented cousin into the room with Fox. The man ran at George and struck him a terrible blow with both hands. George resisted only by standing ramrod still. He noticed Keate standing at the door and called out, "Keate, dost thou allow this?"

Keate only smiled and nodded.

"Is this manly or civil," asked George between blows, for he would do nothing to harm his attacker, "to have us under a guard and then put a man to abuse and beat us? Is this manly or civil or Christian?"

Keate made no reply, but simply moved aside when

constables, brought in by the other Friends, saved Fox from further injury.

The soldiers soon became embarrassed by Keate's open hatred. Besides, they were not sure, at this point, if George was a witch or a man of God. Either way, they were beginning to feel that he was not someone to trifle with. But in the next town, Captain Keate tried again. He separated the Quakers, putting Fox into a room with an armed man.

Fox, starting into the room, drew back and bellowed out: "What now, Keate; what trick hast thou played now, to put me into a room where there is a man with his naked rapier? What is thy end in this?"

Keate tried to quiet him. "Oh pray hold your tongue; for if you speak to this man, we cannot rule him he is so devilish."

George, knowing his only safety lay in drawing attention to the trick, would not hold his tongue. He shouted, "What an unworthy, base trick is this?" His bellowings, in that voice used to reaching hundreds of people in outdoor meetings, soon alerted the troopers. George was immediately placed in the room with the other prisoners.

The next day, Captain Keate finally delivered his charges to the Launceston jail. It was difficult to say who was happier to part company—the soldiers or the Quakers.

For nine weeks the Quakers were kept in jail. By the time the trial came, a large crowd had gathered and was hoping for a hanging. The mob was so unruly that the sheriff's men had to keep the people from grabbing the prisoners as they were marched through the streets to the courthouse.

Why such a crowd? If theological debating was a sport, it was a bloodless one. And there was nothing the seventeenth century Englishmen liked better than a blood sport. Public hangings and witch burnings filled this need. Families often picnicked beneath a row of freshly executed prisoners on gibbets; parents took their young children to see a witch being burned at the stake.

The trial started badly enough. True to their principles, the Friends would not remove their hats when Sir John Glynne, the ruling judge, entered the court.

"The court *commands* you to put off your hats," said Glynne, full of superfluous dignity.

Fox refused. He also refused to remain silent. "Where did ever any magistrate, king, or judge, from Moses to Daniel, command any to put off their hats when they came before him in his court, either amongst the Jews, the people of God, or amongst the heathen?" (This appeal to Old Testament precedent was common in Puritan trials.) "And if the law of England doth command any such thing, show me that law either written or printed."

Angrily, Glynne retorted, "I do not carry my law books on my back."

But Fox pressed him. "Tell me where it is printed in any statute book, that I may read it."

Sir John was so livid at being put on the spot that he completely lost his temper. "Take him away," he shouted.

The courtroom was cleared.

When he had recovered his temper, Glynne reconvened the court, resolved to catch George at his own game. He looked slyly at Fox. "Come," he said, "where had they hats from Moses to Daniel?" He grinned. "I have you fast now."

But he did not have Fox at all. Pointing to Daniel 3:21, Fox said that the three children of Israel were "cast into the fiery furnace . . . with their coats, their hose, and their hats on."

Sir John was furious. "Take them away, jailer."

In jail the Quakers sought to pass the time by reading. But to further harass them, Judge Glynne sent a soldier to confiscate their books. So Fox turned to writing. It was something he frequently did in jail. Somehow he always managed to get paper and pens in prison. (Writing letters and books is a time-honored way for religious prisoners to spend their hours, from John Bunyan to Daniel Berrigan.) Fox addressed a paper against swearing to the juries, and it found its way into Sir John's hands.

When the court was finally reconvened, the first thing Glynne did was to have this paper presented to George, and he asked if Fox had written that seditious document.

George knew that if the paper were heard by the jury, it would clear him of all the charges. The letter also fully explained his position on the Oath of Abjuration. However, if the paper were not read in open court, George doubted that the jury would ever hear it. So he refused to take the document from the clerk, saying that if the clerk read it aloud he would be able to tell if it were his or not. Since Sir John could not force Fox to read the paper himself, he at last gave the clerk permission to read it out loud. The clerk barely finished it when George claimed it as his own.

But the harassment was far from ended. Judge Glynne again ordered the Quakers to remove their hats. He even went so far as to have their hats removed for them. But the Friends calmly put the hats back on again. As he placed his hat upon his head, George turned to Glynne and said, "For what cause have we lain in prison these nine weeks, seeing that thee objects to nothing but our hats?"

The cause, it seemed, was a charge of high treason. It had been brought by none other than Peter Ceely, the justice from Ives. Ceely was playing a double role in the trial. He was not only the accuser, he was also one of the justices sitting on the court. He claimed that Fox had approached him with a plan to raise 40,000 men in an hour's time to push the country into another civil war to bring in the Catholic monarch, Charles of France.

"He told me," recalled Ceely, "how serviceable I might be for his design." Ceely went on to say that he had refused to turn traitor, offering instead to spirit Fox out of the country. "Furthermore," said Ceely, "if it please you, my lord, I have a witness to swear it."

Before the witness could be called, George rose up to object to the procedures. After all, he was not on trial for plotting against the Commonwealth. He insisted the original charges be read and that he be tried on them, as was his right.

"It shall not be read," said Glynne.

"It ought to be," said Fox, and turned to one of his fellow prisoners who happened to have a copy of the charges with him—just in case.

"It shall not be read," declared the judge loudly. And he added in a shout, "Jailer, take him away."

For the third time since the start of the trial, George was taken away.

But the trial had to continue. It was already more than nine weeks old and pressure was brought to bear on the judge to finish it. So Fox was quickly recalled and the original charges were read. They consisted of the following: "Hav[ing] spread several papers tending to the disturbance of the public peace, and cannot render any lawful cause for coming into these parts, being persons altogether unknown, having no pass for travelling up and down the country, and refusing to give sureties for their good behaviour . . . and refus[ing] to take the oath of abjuration."

In other words, they were being charged with the equivalent of disturbing the peace, vagrancy, crossing state lines to incite a riot, and refusing to take a loyalty oath. These, plus the continual "contempt of court"— not removing their hats, talking out of turn, insisting on papers being read, knowing more Bible than the judges—were the total sum of the real charges. The treason charge was simply added on when it was clear that no one took the other charges seriously.

Fox was his own lawyer. He pointed out that if Ceely had indeed offered to get him out of the country instead of immediately turning him in, Ceely was as guilty as Fox. Besides, it had taken over two months before these "charges" had been brought to light.

Even Judge Glynne could see that the treason charge was sheer nonsense. It was dropped.

However, Sir John had the final say. He fined the three Quakers twenty marks apiece for not putting off their hats, and sentenced them to Launceston jail until the fine was paid.

Because Fox and his companions would not pay the jailer his fee, he put them into a "nasty, stinking" part of Launceston jail called Doomsdale, from which very few prisoners ever returned with their health intact.

Doomsdale had a horrible reputation, and George's description does nothing to enhance it. The Quakers had no beds, and no food except what their friends could bring them. Those friends were as likely to be arrested for visiting them as not.

There was no bathroom in the place, and the dirt floor was ankle-deep in rot, slime, and excrement from the previous inmates. When the Quakers tried to burn bits of straw to take away the intolerable smell, the jailer tossed a full chamber pot on them from the floor above.

George and his companions drew up a paper protesting their condition and sent it by one of their visitors to the judges, with a copy to Cromwell. The judges, horrified as much by the outcry as by the conditions of the jail, had Doomsdale opened up and cleaned. And Cromwell, himself, ordered an investigation of the trial.

While the Quakers lay in Doomsdale, an unknown Friend went to the Lord Protector and offered himself, body for body, to stay in prison in Fox's stead. He was willing, if necessary, to die there for George. Cromwell explained that he could not, by law, allow such an exchange. But the Friend's gesture so moved him that he remarked to his council, "Which of you would do as much for me if I were in the same condition?"

> As I passed [James Nayler], I cast
> my eye upon him and a fear struck me
> concerning him.
>
> —GEORGE FOX, *Journal*

Chapter 10

The Fall of James Nayler

It was a beautiful September day in 1656 when Fox and his companions were set free from Doomsdale. After days of wrangling with the authorities about the terms of their release, Fox and the other two Friends were finally freed without any conditions at all. It was a singular triumph for the Quakers.

Furthermore, in many parts of England, the Children of the Light were being allowed to speak at markets or at churches without being officially harassed. It was as though by investigating the circumstances of George's trial and by speaking well of him personally, Cromwell had endorsed the Quaker movement.

It would have been a perfect new beginning for the

Friends in that Fall of 1656 but for one man. James Nayler.

James Nayler was one of the original Publishers of Truth. He had been with Fox at Swarthmore Hall when George had first met the Fells. Nayler was a man of great physical beauty. His shoulder-length red-brown hair framed a rawboned yet aesthetic-looking face that was set off by a spiked beard. His speeches were known for their passionate intensity and great persuasiveness. His written letters and pamphlets were praised for their beauty of language and sincerity of thought. Nayler was indeed one of the brightest of the Quaker stars.

But James Nayler was also, in Fox's words, a man who had "run out into imaginations"; a man who, when overworked both physically and spiritually, was to have a mental breakdown that would greatly endanger the young and growing Quaker movement.

When Fox, Pyot, and their companion were in Doomsdale, Nayler and twenty-one other Friends had tried to visit them. For their pains, the visitors had been put in prison themselves, so that when Fox was released he visited Nayler in jail and not the other way around.

The twenty-one Friends with whom Nayler had been jailed included nine women. Among them were Hannah Stranger, Martha Simonds, and Dorcas Erbury, who claimed that Nayler had raised her from the dead. These three women were all hysterics, given to rambling, passionate speech. And they all worshiped

Nayler. For example, Hannah Stranger insisted on calling him "the fairest of ten thousand" and "the only begotten Son of God."

George, of course, had heard rumors of Nayler's strange band of followers and greatly disapproved of them. When he visited Nayler in prison, their meeting was a strained one. Fox was already weakened by his own harsh imprisonment. When Nayler, in the manner of the day, tried to embrace him, he offered Nayler his boot to kiss, saying, "James, it will be harder for thee to get down thy rude company than it was for thee to set them up."

It is hard to understand why George was so unfeeling towards Nayler. It must have been obvious that Nayler was a deeply disturbed man. The strain of his ministry, the persecutions and imprisonments, had worked upon his overly-imaginative mind. The attentions of his flatterers, and especially the worshiping women, had begun to convince Nayler that he was, as they said, Jesus returned in the flesh.

Fox was short with him, even harsh. He had been himself in prison, and seen many Quakers die for the truth. He could not be compassionate to Nayler, for he honestly did not recognize that the man was unhinged by misery. George, who would have died—and did suffer—gladly in God's service, saw only a blasphemer, a man who twisted the idea of the Inner Light to his own ends. Fox felt that Nayler had betrayed the Quaker cause, and he also felt personally betrayed by his old friend.

Nayler represented a special problem for Fox and the Quakers. His belief in his own divinity came directly from his belief in the Inner Light. He truly thought that God was telling him—and telling his followers—that he was the Christ returned.

This distortion of the Inner Light was a danger that George had not foreseen. He had not made it clear enough to those he had convinced that God was not speaking through an infallible mechanical instrument which only reproduced God's voice. God was speaking through the very fallible human heart. And when God speaks through the human heart, something of the person who carries the message is bound to intrude. An unbalanced mind could, in fact, distort God's word.

And distort the message was precisely what James Nayler was doing. Fox saw this clearly. So clearly that when he came from visiting Nayler in prison, George said, "As I passed him, I cast my eye upon him and a fear struck me concerning him."

That fear was soon to be justified.

In October 1656, a strange procession made its way towards Bristol. It was the newly-released Nayler and a band of eight Quakers. They were all mad.

Nayler rode upon a horse, his hatted head bowed, his hands folded in prayer. Surrounding him, in various stages of undress, were seven men and women on foot, slogging through the muddy cartways and puddle-filled roads. At the head of the procession, leading the horse by the bridle, were Hannah Stranger and Martha Simonds. Occasionally they would let go of the bridle and fling down their garments or bunches of wildflowers in the mud before the horse so it might step on them instead of the water. All the while, the strange, mad company—with the exception of the praying Nayler—sang "Hosannah! Holy, holy, holy, Lord God of Sabaoth."

If anyone along the way jeered or asked questions, they were answered with songs, wild songs of praise and hallelujahs. Without hesitating, the odd processional kept up through the rain and the mud towards the town of Bristol.

It was an insane parody of Christ's entry into Jerusalem, for those crazed followers had convinced both themselves and Nayler that he was the Son of God. Hannah Stranger's husband had even written to Nayler that "Thy name shall be no more James Nayler but Jesus," a letter which was, for some insane reason, tucked in Nayler's pocket as he made his Triumphant Entry into Bristol on October 24, 1656.

The company started to make their way towards St. Mary Redcliffe Church. At the High Cross, they were met by the sheriff's men and dragged away to prison, to the jeering of an enormous crowd.

What the group needed was compassion, understanding, and a long rest. What they received was incomprehensible, even by seventeenth century standards. The company was dismissed except for Nayler. He alone was brought before Parliament and convicted of blasphemy, not only because of the mad procession, but also on the strong evidence of the Stranger

letter which was found in his pocket. Nayler missed the
death sentence by a small vote: 82–96. But it might
have been preferred to the sentence he did receive. It
was one of the most brutal and bloody ever passed
down by the British House of Commons. It was not
only unconstitutional, it was also against Cromwell's
wishes. And all for what was essentially a mad man's
bit of rococo role-playing.

On December 16, James Nayler heard his sentence.
He was to be pilloried for two hours, half-naked in the
icy cold. Then he was to be roped to a cart and
dragged through the streets of Bristol while the executioner hit him more than 300 times with a knotted
whip. A week after the whipping, he was pilloried
again, and one of his not-so-helpful followers placed a
sign above his head which read "This is the King of
the Jews." The letter B, for blasphemer, was branded
on his forehead with a red-hot iron, and a hole pierced
through his tongue with a red-hot wire. Finally, he was
committed to solitary confinement and hard labor for
as long as Parliament wished. They wished it for three
years.

In all the time of Nayler's imprisonment, Fox refused to forgive him, though many other Quaker leaders begged him to.

The brutal sentence brought Nayler back to his
senses. In fact, when he heard the sentence passed, he
said, "God has given me a body; God will, I hope, give
me a spirit to endure it. The Lord lay not these things
to your charge."

Throughout his long sentence, Nayler never lost hope that he and Fox would be reconciled. Immediately upon his release, he sought George out to beg his forgiveness. Fox was so ill at the time that he could not see Nayler, but Nayler remained patient. Finally, when Fox recovered, they met in London at a large meeting in which the repentant Nayler made a public confession of his errors. Fox rose and embraced Nayler and "healed up the breach" while many of the Friends present wept.

A few months later, in the autumn of 1660, while making a walking tour from London to his Yorkshire home, Nayler was set upon by robbers. They tied him up and left him to die. He was found some time later by Friends, but this last blow was too much for him. James Nayler died, not yet forty-five years old.

About two hours before he died, Nayler spoke a farewell that is considered one of the most beautiful speeches from the early Quaker movement. It showed how completely his radiant spirit had returned and how he was over his madness forever.

There is a spirit which I feel that delights to do no evil nor to revenge any wrong, but delights to endure all things, in hope to enjoy its own in the end. Its hope is to outlive all wrath and contention, and to weary out all exaltation and cruelty, or whatever is of a nature contrary to itself. It sees to the end of all temptations. As it bears no evil in itself, so it conceives none in thoughts to any other. If it be be-

trayed, it bears it, for its crown is meekness, its life is
everlasting love unfeigned; and takes its kingdom
with entreaty and not with contention and keeps it
by lowliness of mind. In God alone it can rejoice,
though none else regard it, or can own its life. It's
conceived in sorrow, and brought forth without any
to pity it, nor doth it murmur at grief and oppres-
sion. It never rejoiceth but through sufferings: for
with the world's joy it is murdered. I found it alone,
being forsaken. I have fellowship therein with them
who lived in dens and desolate places in the earth,
who through death obtained this resurrection and
eternal holy life.

The "fall" of James Nayler, as it is called today, almost dealt a mortal blow to the infant Quaker movement. It had two immediate bad effects: public opin-
ion was entirely against the Quakers, with whom
Nayler was intimately associated, and the Quakers
themselves were frightfully shamed. But in the end it
was a bad cause that had a good effect, for Fox was
forced to be more explicit about what was meant by
the Inner Light of Christ being present in every person. He was forced to see how easily an unbalanced
mind could jump from the notion of the divine light
within to that of its own divinity.

Fox was an idealist, but a practical one. He knew
that he would have to discipline the men and women
in his growing movement. So he began to make them
aware that there can be a higher thing than individual

inspiration—the check and balance of collective inspiration. "Feel the power of God in one another," wrote Fox. And "know one another in this love that changeth not."

This was the beginning of the shift in Quakerism to group mysticism, a change from simple *communion* to *community*. From now on, Fox would write and preach much about unity in prayer, unity with one another, unity with God. This new emphasis saved Quakerism from disappearing into anarchy. Friends all sought to follow the *same* inward light, and in this way come to unity. Fox said it best when he wrote: "The Light is but one; and all being guided by it, all are subject to one, and are one in the unity of the Spirit."

While James Nayler suffered in his solitary prison for three years, George Fox was not still. He had much work to do traveling the length and breadth of England mending the cracks in the Quaker movement, cracks that were in large part brought about by James Nayler's "fall."

The Quaker movement was large enough now so that such cracks caused serious concern. There were so many Quakers in England by 1657 that George could boast: "There are seldom fewer than one thousand in prison in this nation for Truth's sake." But it was not a joyous boast; prison had already made martyrs of too many, including young James Parnell, a gifted young Quaker who had died of starvation in jail some four years earlier.

Fox went from county to county, through Yorkshire, Leicestershire, Staffordshire, Worcestershire, Warwickshire, indeed, as he put it, "having travelled over most of the nation." George always felt that while he traveled he was doing a twofold duty for God—both preaching God's word and setting an example for others to follow. One of the many letters he wrote while in Launceston jail concerned this double quality of traveling: "Let all nations hear the Word by sound or writing," he urged. "Spare no place, spare not tongue nor pen, but be obedient to the Lord God, and go through the world and be valiant for the Truth upon Earth. . . . Be patterns, be examples in all countries, places, islands, nations, wherever you come, that your life may preach among all sorts of people."

Everywhere Fox went, the meetings were large, the convinced Quakers welcoming him with great turnouts and a good deal of religious fervor. Fox was well satisfied with the English Friends. "The Lord's power had surrounded this nation round about as with a wall and bulwark, and His Seed reached from sea to sea."

But it did not actually reach from sea to sea. There was still Wales. And after that, Scotland, if the borders of the island nation were to be reached. So George traveled as a "pattern" in both those countries, bringing many more new Friends to the Quaker way.

Friends did not concern themselves
with the outward powers or governments.
—George Fox, *Journal*

Chapter 11

The Return of the King

Three events in the next three years were to have a great influence on George Fox's life, and two of these were to be felt the world around.

First, in 1658, Judge Fell, that gentle but firm master of Swarthmore Hall, died. Besides losing a high-placed supporter, a Quaker champion in the upper classes and a man who could talk with other justices in their own language, Fox lost a long-time friend. However, Swarthmore Hall remained, by the judge's will, in Margaret Fell's capable hands. She never faltered. In fact, she took so much upon herself that she soon became the backbone of the young Quaker movement as George was its heart.

Judge Fell's death was not the only one to affect George in 1658. That year Oliver Cromwell died, too.

Although George often stated: "Friends did not concern themselves with outward powers and governments," Cromwell's death concerned them a great deal. Cromwell had been blamed by the Quakers for much of the persecutions that had been visited upon them. This was truly ironic. Oliver Cromwell was a man who loved liberty and hated persecutions, particularly religious persecution. But he had been forced to enact rigid laws that were enforced by small, cruel, vindictive people. Such laws, like the Oath of Abjuration designed to flush out Jesuit plotters, were used to persecute religious nonconformists like the Quakers. The Puritans even saw the Quakers' refusal to put off their hats as part of a Jesuit plot. Some Protestants actually believed that the Quaker hats were hiding the shaven crowns of Catholic monks.

Unfortunately, Fox did not understand all the prevailing social, political, and economic conditions in England during the years that he lived. He was narrow-minded in the sense that his eye was firmly fixed on heaven. To him, little else mattered. So he found it hard to forgive a leader, like Cromwell, who was forced to be pragmatic.

When in 1657 there had been talk of making Cromwell king, Fox journeyed to London specifically to advise Cromwell against such a move. He had had a presentment of Cromwell's death, and he said to the Lord

Protector, "They that would put thee on a crown would take away thy life."

If George had understood Cromwell better, he would have realized that the Lord Protector had never been tempted to take the crown. But Fox saw only the outward trappings of power surrounding Cromwell. He did not see that the trappings were also very much a trap; that Cromwell was powerless to make his followers less vindictive in carrying out certain laws. Fox knew that those laws had resulted in the jailing of well over 3,000 Friends—and the beating and torturing and even the deaths of many innocent Quakers. For all this he blamed Cromwell.

The next year, 1658, in London George saw Cromwell riding in Hampton Court and wrote that he felt "a waft of death go forth against him." Later, when he rode up to talk with the Lord Protector, George reported that Cromwell looked like a dead man.

Fox's presentments were correct. On September 3, 1658, Cromwell was dead.

Following his death, the country was in an uproar. At first Cromwell's son tried to rule, but he could not. Waiting in the European wings was Charles Stuart, son of the murdered king. Charles was nominally a Protestant, but he had a Catholic mother, Henrietta Maria, and a Catholic brother, James. The English people were torn. They wanted the return of the king —but at what price?

Whenever there are upheavals in high places, there are mighty echoes of the trouble in low places. Some-

how the Quakers seemed to bear the brunt of the un-
steady times. Their meetings were continually broken
up by violence. One meeting, held seven miles from
London, was visited by an unruly mob that beat up
eighty Friends, including women and children. No one
gave it much thought because it was such a common
occurrence. Meetings were always being broken up—
by a hail of rotten eggs, by drums breaking into the si-
lences, by physical beatings, by jailing.

In all the upheaval, only the Quakers themselves remained calm, Fox the calmest of all. He cautioned
Friends to stay out of the oncoming revolution, to fight
with spiritual weapons only. The Quakers turned their
concern inward, worrying about the care of imprisoned
Friends and their families, petitioning Parliament to
let 164 Friends take the place of an equal number of
sick Quakers in the jails. But always they stayed out of
the larger maelstrom of "outward powers and governments."

At this time, which was also when James Nayler was
about to be released from prison, George became seriously ill. For ten weeks he was semiconscious. Friends
feared he would die. Although there were physical as-
pects of his disease—he lost weight, he had fits of chok-
ing, his face grew thin and wan—it is clear that it was
brought on by overwork and fatigue. Certainly it was
aggravated by the fear that the change in government
might mean even further persecutions for the growing
Quaker movement, which now numbered 40,000
Friends. Whether he liked to admit it or not, Fox was

worldly enough to know what such a change *could* mean.

The Puritans under Cromwell were Protestants who, outwardly at least, believed in freedom of religion. Like the Quakers they were against the flighty, gay, worldly life of a king's court. Their eyes were on heaven as much as George Fox's were. (Unlike the Quakers, though, they believed that authority rested in Scripture and that the paid priests were its proper interpreters.) A restored king might not only bring back the hated Catholic religion, but reinstitute the worldly pleasures of court life as well.

On the other hand, the Puritans called themselves saints while surrounding themselves with the trappings of power. They spoke of religious freedom, but in fact the only religion that was free was their own. Cromwell was friendly towards George Fox and had done nothing to encourage persecution. He also had done nothing to stop it.

Meanwhile, from Breda in Holland, the exiled Charles Stuart had issued a declaration on liberty of conscience that claimed in part: "no man shall be . . . called in question for differences of opinions in matters of religion."

Which would be better for the Quakers—the self-proclaimed Puritan saints who denied sanctity to others or the worldly, pleasure-seeking king who talked of religious freedom? It was indeed a puzzle, and George Fox puzzled it over and over until he became very sick.

Neither Fox's illness nor the reluctance of Friends to commit themselves to one side or the other affected in any real way the history that was being made. Force of arms did—Charles Stuart's force of arms. They brought him victorious into England on May 8, 1660, where he was proclaimed Charles II.

Because of the Declaration of Breda, and because Charles II already had a reputation as a fair man who understood the common people (understandably since he had spent much of his young life in impoverished exile, often disguised as a servant), Fox was hopeful about the new regime.

But in the very first year of the new king's reign, Fox was again thrown into prison. What George had not taken into account was the weathercocking ability of the people in power. Many of those who had been the Quakers' chief persecutors under Cromwell had switched sides at the right moment and were in a position, under the Restoration, to persecute them again.

This time, Fox was arrested right in Swarthmore Hall, something that never would have happened had Judge Fell been alive. The constables came into the Hall on the pretext of "searching for arms." They claimed that it was known that the Quakers were trying to start a rebellion against the king. (Two years earlier, the Friends were being charged with plotting against Cromwell. It was different, yet it was still the same.)

When the constables came upon George, they laid hold of him and shouted that he was the very man they had been looking for—arms indeed! They took him at once to the home of the Ulverston chief constable under a guard of sixteen men. During the long night, while Fox slept peacefully, the guard stayed awake. Some of them even sat in the chimney, for fear Fox would escape up it.

These new kingsmen were as afraid of Fox as the old Cromwellians had been. Small wonder since they were the same people, only with different uniforms. One soldier said he did not think 1,000 men would have been able to capture Fox if they hadn't come upon him by accident at Swarthmore Hall. Yet it seems strange that so much force was necessary against a man who had always refused to lift his hand against anyone.

The next morning, the guards searched George and were careful to remove his pocketknife and spurs. Then they seated him on a small pony instead of his own fast horse.

Barely out of town, the company was met by Margaret Fell and her daughters who had come to say farewell to Fox. The constables immediately circled around George, shouting, "Will they rescue him? Will they rescue him?" If it hadn't been so serious, it would have been funny. George, seeing how frightened they were, said, "Here is my hair; here is my back; here are my cheeks; strike on."

Fox's manner shamed the guards. They meekly led his horse away and crossed the Morecambe sands to Lancaster. Evidently the word that Fox had been captured had already spread through the town. The streets were crowded with onlookers. As the company of constables and their prisoner rode through the town, Fox looked around at the crowd. Someone called out, "Look at his eyes," and the noisy mob was immediately sobered. Many looked away.

The reason Fox was thrown into prison this time is unclear. Disloyalty to the king was alleged, but never proven. In jail awaiting trial, George wrote a letter to the new king saying: "We . . . utterly deny . . . all outward wars and strife and fightings with outward weapons, for any end or under any pretence whatsoever . . . and we do certainly know, and so testify to the world, that the spirit of Christ, which leads us into all Truth, will never move us to fight and war against any man with outward weapons, neither for the kingdom of Christ, nor for the kingdoms of this world." The letter remains the main Quaker position on war to this day.

Evidently King Charles believed Fox. For when he was visited by Margaret Fell and Ann Curtis, whose father had been hanged by Cromwellians for supporting the king during the days of the Commonwealth, Charles sent a letter to Lancaster ordering Fox to be let out on bail.

Fox returned for his trial and spoke so convincingly of his innocence—pointing out that not only had his accuser never shown up in court, but that King Charles himself had faith enough in his innocence to urge his release—that George was set free. He had already served twenty weeks in the Lancaster jail.

The king then swore that no one would molest the Friends again so long as they lived peacefully.

Fox believed him, just as he had at first believed Cromwell.

What I am in words, I am the same in life.
            —GEORGE FOX, *Journal*

Chapter 12

Restoration–the Renewal of Persecution

In many ways, George Fox was an innocent. When he said "Verily" there was no altering him, even as a boy. As he told one persecutor, "What I am in words, I am the same in life." He expected other people to be just as straight and as truthful. If the king said that "none should molest [the Quakers] so long as [they] live peaceably," Fox considered that nothing needed to be added. The king's word was good, and the king's word was law.

As if to underline such a notion, Charles had released 700 Friends jailed in Cromwell's time. There were some Quakers now in Parliament, and from that august forum they were able to explain why the

Friends were against certain religious institutions such as a paid priesthood, tithing, formal church services, and the sacraments.

However, the king's word had to be executed by the king's men. Not all of them were as amicable to the Friends as was Charles himself. Furthermore, the king, unlike Fox, often altered his word—depending upon circumstances. Scarcely had his promise been given to the Quakers when it was taken back—because of circumstances. A paper drawn up to give the Quakers complete freedom of worship was waiting on the king's desk ready to be signed, when a plot by the Fifth Monarchy Men to depose the king was discovered.

The Fifth Monarchy Men were religious fanatics who expected Christ to return momentarily, and to England. They wanted to set up the Fifth Monarchy on the British Isles (the first four having been the Assyrian, Persian, Greek, and Roman empires). And they were against both the ruling civil and church governments.

Unfortunately, the plot was laid mostly at Quaker feet. All that the Friends had in common with the Fifth Monarchy Men was a desire to worship outside the established church and a disinterest in either church or civil powers. But the Quakers would not have taken part in a bloody uprising such as the Fifth Monarchists were sponsoring. They were, as George was fond of saying, "peaceable people." Yet because they were a highly visible group, refusing to hide their meetings, they were the ones accused of plotting against the king.

Charles never signed the freedom-of-religion paper waiting on his desk. But that was not all. Friends were taken prisoner at their meetings the first Sunday (or "First Day" as they called it) after the plot was discovered. Some 4,200 Quakers were hauled off to jail because of the Fifth Monarchy plot, 500 in London alone. In Cambridge, all the Quakers were sent to prison, including the smallest children. As George Whitehead, one of the jailed Friends, wrote: "The sudden storm swept many counties bare of men Friends."

George was swept up along with them. He was arrested Saturday evening by soldiers who shouted that he was "one of the heads, and a chief ringleader." It was only through the intervention of Richard Marche, a Lord of the King's Bedchamber, that George was not immediately jailed.

The Fifth Monarchy plot was not really a serious threat. Still, coming as soon as it did after the restoration of the king, it seemed more serious than it was. The country became paralyzed by a wave of fear, and on the heels of that fear came violence. Rioters tore through the cities, honest wayfarers were stopped and searched by soldiers on any excuse.

When Fox was jailed, Margaret Fell undertook several journeys on his behalf to plead personally with King Charles. At the same time, George wrote a declaration and had it published in the papers, a declaration that came out against both the plotting and fighting, and also the jailing of innocent Friends. The declaration was read in high places. Even the king saw a copy. So when Margaret went to plead for George's case, her pleas did not fall on completely deaf ears. Charles issued an order to stop the illegal search and seizure. Any soldiers would now have to be accompanied by a constable if they wanted to search a home. This was a kind of guaranty, like a search warrant, that nothing illegal would take place.

But that did not clear the jails of the innocent religious prisoners. In fact the jails did not offer up the Friends until the real plotters were led away to execution. At that time, under what they considered the Eye of God, the Fifth Monarchy Men absolved the Quakers of any complicity in the conspiracy. Relieved, King Charles set the imprisoned Quakers free.

However, much damage had already been done, and not only to the health and well-being of the imprisoned Friends and their families. Mobs had been regularly breaking up Quaker meetings all over England. The stores and homes belonging to jailed Quakers were ransacked by thieves who openly carted away cattle, household goods, food, clothing, blankets, and beds.

In America, where the first Quaker preachers had gone in 1656, things were even worse. Because they preached that each man had to answer to the "Light Within," the Quakers were considered anarchists. In Massachusetts, for example, Quakers were banished and could only return on pain of death. Already four Friends—Mary Dyer, William Robinson, Marmaduke Stephenson, and William Leddra—had been hanged on Boston Common.

This bloody American practice came to the king's attention when the Quakers were declared innocent of the Fifth Monarchy plot. Friend Edward Burrough told Charles: "There is a vein of innocent blood opened in your dominion which if it were not stopped would overrun all."

Charles replied, "But I will stop that vein."

"Then do it speedily," said Burrough, "for we do not know how many may soon be put to death."

Charles called for his secretary at once and, while Burrough watched, dictated a royal order to stop the slaughter and jailing of American innocents.

Besides putting an end to the American persecutions, Charles delivered up hundreds of Friends imprisoned under Cromwell and absolved the Quakers of any involvement with the Fifth Monarchy Men.

But Charles did other things as well, things which were inharmonious with his good acts. He let Parliament have its way on major religious issues. Under the circumstances of his shaky return to the English throne, he could do nothing else. Parliament passed the Act of Uniformity in 1662. As its name indicates, it was hard on religious dissenters. The law ruled that the clergy had to consent to everything found in the Book of Common Prayer of the English Church. Two thousand dissenting Puritan preachers were immediately ejected from their pulpits. While this Act did not directly affect the Quakers, who had neither clergy nor any claims to being part of the English Church, it certainly indicated the country's mood.

Then, in 1664, the Conventicle Act was passed, an act that struck directly at the Friends. No more than five people were allowed to gather at a meeting other than a Church of England service. For first offenders, there was a fine of five pounds ($25), quite a large sum in those days. The second offense commanded a ten pounds ($50) fine or six months imprisonment. Anyone arrested a third time under this Act was deported to a foreign plantation. It was an unnecessarily cruel and harsh law enacted specifically to stop the Quaker meetings. These persecuting laws of the Restoration were known collectively as the Clarendon Code.

Needless to say, the Quakers refused to obey these laws which they considered illegal, immoral, and unjust. They practiced what is now called civil disobedience. They continued to meet in groups as large as might be collected whenever the Spirit moved them. They never held these meetings secretly, but were always open in both the calling and the holding of their meetings.

The authorities found it almost impossible to deal with a group of people who not only had no fear of imprisonment, but more important, felt that the rule of the conscience was the only law to be obeyed. What could the constables do to them? Arrest the minister and thus break up the meeting? There was no minister. Arrest all the men? The women, equal in all things, carried on. Arrest all the men *and* all the women? In Bristol and in Reading the constables did just this and the children continued the meetings by themselves for many weeks.

Still, the arrests went on. During the first two years of the Restoration alone, more than 3,000 Friends were imprisoned. By 1689, 12,000 more had been in jail. Over 300 died in their cells.

And George Fox was imprisoned again, too.

Swear not at all.
                              —JESUS, in Matthew 5:34

Swear not, neither by heaven, neither
by the earth, neither by any other oath: but
let your yea be yea; and your nay, nay.
                              —Epistle of James 5:12

Chapter 13

The Longest Imprisonment

Harassed by the Conventicle and Uniformity Acts, and at a time when they most needed Fox's strong guiding hand or at least Margaret Fell's never-wavering faith and love, the Quakers were suddenly bereft of their leaders. Within months of one another, George and Mistress Fell were both cast into prison.

In the autumn of 1663, George came back to Swarthmore Hall from a preaching trip. He found the manor house in an uproar. Chests and trunks had been overturned. Doors flung open. Beds ripped apart. Desks and tables all but destroyed. An officer sent by Colonel Kirkby of Kirkby Hall had been searching the house, looking for treasonable material and Quaker leaders.

Fox might have fled, for there was plenty of time for escape. Instead, he rode to Kirkby Hall, five miles distant. George arrived just in time for a farewell party for the colonel who was leaving next day for London to serve in Parliament.

Kirkby was obviously embarrassed by Fox's presence in front of his guests. He mumbled that he had nothing personal against George. But Mistress Fell, he said, "must not keep great meetings at her house, for they are contrary to the Act."

George replied that the Act was not meant to apply to the peaceful Quaker meetings which were for worship, but rather for those who met "to plot and contrive and raise insurrections against the King."

Kirkby agreed. But they both knew that the Act was really being used to harass the Quakers who had made the mistake of becoming too successful. The established church, fearing a religion based purely on the Spirit would lead not only to anarchy but a loss of the church's money and its privileged place in society, had sought alliance with the state to supplement its own authority. The Church of England encouraged the official persecution.

However, though Kirkby knew all this, he certainly could not admit it. So he repeated, "I have nothing against you." He even shook Fox's hand.

George returned to Swarthmore Hall elated, to set the house aright. He felt he had won a victory. In fact, he had won nothing at all. A few weeks later, the local justices, with the tacit approval of Kirkby in London, decided to arrest Fox.

By some Quaker underground spy system, George heard of their decision in plenty of time to make his escape. But he did not run away. As he put it, "I considered that . . . if I should go away they might fall upon Friends; but if I gave up myself to be taken away, it might stop them, and Friends would escape the better." As always, George put the good of others before his own safety.

When an armed officer came the next day to arrest him, George met him at the door. He said, "I am ready." Accompanied by the ever-faithful Margaret Fell, Fox went off with the officer to Holker Hall where he was to be examined. It turned out to be only the first in a long series of farcical trials that lasted fourteen months. All but three of those months Fox spent in jail.

Fox was questioned at Holker Hall for many hours by a panel of judges. At first he answered their questions serenely. They were no different from the queries he was asked by priests and justices every day. But when one of the judges called him a traitor and a rebel, George lost his temper. He slammed his fist upon the table. He told them loudly that he had served six months in Derby prison because he would *not* take up arms against the king. He reminded them forcefully how he had been accused of treason by the Cromwellians in 1654 and jailed for it. "For ye talk of the King, a company of you. But where were ye in Oliver's days, and what did ye do then for him?"

It was a good question to put to that "company" of weathercocking justices, for many of them had been judges under Cromwell, serving him as loyally as they now claimed they served the king. It was such a good question that they immediately changed the subject. The queries turned to the Monarchy Men Plot. But George defended himself so well on that old charge that Judge Middleton in exasperation called, "Bring the book [the Bible] and put the oaths of allegiance and supremacy to him."

It was a final effort on Middleton's part. Having no real charges to bring against Fox, he turned to the sure-fire Quaker-catcher. No Friend would swear an oath.

Instead of putting George in jail, though, the judges announced that they considered him guilty and that he would have to be tried by the assize court in Lancaster the following January.

That January trial was almost a rerun of all previous Quaker trials. Hat on head, George entered the courtroom. The presiding judge told him to remove his hat and George refused. The judge asked how Fox intended to show respect to the justices if he would not remove his hat. Fox replied simply and sincerely, "In coming when they called me." As usual, he had gone straight to the heart of the matter.

Again, these judges asked George to swear the oath. Again he refused. So he was committed to prison until he might be tried by a jury, three months hence.

It was during George's long trial that Margaret Fell

was also sent to prison, on the same charges. Her sentence was *praemunire,* an especially harsh one for landholders. It meant that she was considered outlawed from the king's protection: all her lands, goods, and money were forfeited to the crown. She had to remain in prison for as long as the king wished. It was a heavy blow because it meant that Swarthmore Hall itself was in jeopardy. As she was led off to jail, Margaret remarked, "Although I am out of the king's protection, yet I am not out of the protection of the Almighty God."

Three months later, Fox again came to trial, having lain all that time in a filthy, pestilent prison. But when the charge against him was read, Fox took a long time pointing out the many errors in it. There were enough errors to set him free on technicalities. The day of his trial was recorded incorrectly, the year of the king's reign was wrong. Both of these mistakes raised doubt as to whether the trial had even occurred. Furthermore, George was not even properly identified as an English subject. After all, only a subject of the English king need swear allegiance to him.

The enormity of the errors caused the judge to agree that George should be freed. There was no time for rejoicing, though, for the judge immediately added in a rage, "But then, *I* can put the oath to any man here, and I will tender you the oath again." He had the Bible brought in for George to swear on.

Fox stood rigid. "If it be a Bible, give it me into my hand."

There was immediate silence in the court. Would the "Pope of the North," as Fox was often called, actually swear?

George picked up the Bible and opened it. "I see it is a Bible and am glad of it," he said and nodded. Every eye was on him. George had a sure sense of drama. He turned and stared at the judge, and the judge finally looked away with a red face.

Hesitantly the clerk read the oath and the judge asked Fox to swear it.

"Ye have given me a book here to kiss and swear on," George began, looking around at his stilled audience. "And [in] this book which ye have given me to kiss . . . the Son says 'Swear not at all! . . .' Now I say as the book says, and yet ye imprison me. Why do ye not imprison the book?"

Shocked silence. Then several small laughs which threatened to engulf the courtroom. The furious judge grabbed the Bible from George's hands. "Nay, but we *will* imprison George Fox!"

They did imprison Fox, but his "Why do ye not imprison the book?" became a byword to mock the oath from then on.

All in all, the various judges tried six different times to get Fox to take the oath. Why was he so rigid on the subject of swearing? It was because, as he said, "our Yea is yea, and our Nay is nay, and if we transgress our yea and nay, let us suffer as they do . . . that swear falsely." He based his argument on Scripture. In the Sermon on the Mount, Christ said, "Swear not at all."

James, in an epistle, enlarged on that simple statement: "Swear not, neither by heaven, neither by the
earth, neither by any other oath. . . ." The simplicity
of the truth was what George and the Quakers were
after. As William Penn's epigram put it: "People swear
to the end they may speak truth; Christ would have
them speak truth to the end they might not swear."

The prison cell that George was committed to was
the worst he had been in. He was in the tower at Lancaster prison, where the smoke from the other prisoners' fires stood "as heavy as dew on walls." It rained on
his bed and the high cell was open to the wind. Fox
was half-starved and frozen with the cold. His body
was constantly swollen and his limbs so benumbed that
he developed arthritis, though he was only thirty-nine
years old. He lay in the cold, wet cell all winter waiting
for a new trial. The miracle was that he did not die.

In March he was brought out for yet another trial.
Again the charge was full of errors. When George
pointed out the errors, the presiding judge was so
angry that he had Fox removed from the courtroom
and sentenced him *in absentia,* an absolutely illegal pro-
cedure.

Back in Lancaster prison, weakened in body but not
in spirit ("The Truth can live in the gaols," he wrote)
George began having visions again, the first he had
had since he began his ministry. He foresaw the defeat
of the Turks, the wars with Holland, the great London
Fire. And he wrote continuously with his swollen,

numb hands: letters, articles, pamphlets.

Meanwhile, the justices in Lancaster were not happy with Fox's presence. He had many supporters in the area. Even those people who were not Quakers had been impressed with the way he had carried himself throughout the long series of trials. The judges discussed moving him to another prison, one farther from his friends. Kirkby even suggested Fox be sent "beyond seas."

At last, in April 1665, the troopers were ordered to remove the sick Fox from Lancaster prison. Their destination was the East coast of England. George was to be sent to Scarborough Castle, a 500-year-old fortress on the Yorkshire Moors, overlooking the sea.

Fox was so weak from lying in the cold, wet Lancaster prison for a year, he could barely stand. Yet he stood up to the troopers who came for him, asking to see their orders, refusing to drink their wine. They lifted him bodily on to a horse and strapped him there, for he could never have sat upon it alone. Then they rode him at a rapid pace through town. One young trooper kept whipping the horse to make it rear and bolt. Then he would ride ahead and ask Fox mockingly, "How do you do, Mr. Fox?"

Friends had somehow heard of the move, and there was a company of silent Quakers to meet Fox on the road and lend him encouragement. But it frightened the troopers, who milled about the sick horseman uncertainly. Since there was no move to rescue the prisoner, the troopers finally became bolder and escorted

George on down the road. After several hard days of riding, they came at last to the seaside castle that was to be Fox's new home.

Again, Fox was put in horrible quarters, worse even than the Lancaster cell. This imprisonment, coming after the hard ride and year-long confinement in Lancaster, nearly killed him and he never after enjoyed that wonderful vigorous strength for which he had been known.

The Scarborough cell was tiny. The sea winds and rain came through openings in the walls—probably the old arrow slits. George was able to plug up the worst of them. But no sooner had he made his cell slightly more livable than the jailers moved him to an even smaller room. Here the sea winds constantly chilled him. He was wet day and night from the harsh northern rains. He rarely had a fire. Often he had only a three-penny loaf of bread, weak beer, and fetid water to keep him from starvation. The bread had to last as long as three weeks. It was not imprisonment—it was slow death.

Although Fox was allowed no Quaker visitors, there was a constant stream of others—priests, college professors, university graduates. They all came to pester the infamous George Fox, trying to prove to him why he should swear an oath. While the unfriendly visitors were a trial to George, and he complained about them, in truth they sustained him. They helped keep him alive through the long cold confinement. He took pleasure in debating with all the learned professors. He was proud of how—sick and imprisoned though he was—he could best them in any argument.

By the summer of 1666, many Friends were crowded into prisons or banished. Those jailed in London's Newgate Prison, where the Plague was rampant, died by the hundreds. With so many Quakers in prison, it seemed as though there was no one to ease Fox's confinement.

Yet after almost a year of looking the other way, Sir Jordan Crosslands, Governor of Scarborough Castle, became interested in his famous prisoner. When such a man as Edward Marche (the king's Lord of the Bedchamber) stated he would go a hundred miles barefoot for Fox's liberty, Governor Crosslands began to listen. Soon Crosslands fell under Fox's powerful personality. He allowed George to write a letter to the king, since only Charles could set aside the conviction.

Marche carried the letter personally to King Charles, who—to his credit—seemed genuinely surprised that Fox was still in prison. Such was the chaotic state in those days that Charles had lost sight of the imprisoned Quaker.

Charles immediately sent a letter releasing Fox from Scarborough. Upon its receipt, Crosslands let Fox go free. He was released on September 1, 1666, the day before the great London Fire that destroyed St. Paul's Church and 13,000 houses.

The soldiers and officers who had guarded George while he was a prisoner gave him one of the greatest accolades of his life. They said, "He was as stiff as a tree, and as pure as a bell, for we could never bow him."

In journeys often . . . in prison more frequent.

—GEORGE FOX, *Journal*

Chapter 14

United in the Seed

Almost twenty years had passed since George Fox first began spreading the word about the Inner Light. Twenty years is a generation. In that time, a child born of converted parents, a birthright Friend, would have grown up.

Many of the fiery, older preachers, the original Publishers of Truth, were dead: Aldam, Caton, Nayler, Farnsworth. Others had crossed the seas. Still others were currently in jail, or had suffered health-breaking imprisonment.

The new, younger generation of Friends was quieter, more sophisticated, more educated, dealing less in open confrontation and more in conversion by reason.

They were conservative in that they wanted to con-
serve—or preserve—those rights already won by their
radical fathers and mothers. Even the new converts
were of a different kind, from higher classes, better
schooled. Two of Quakerism's most eminent converts
had just recently become Friends: William Penn, a
young aristocrat and author, and Robert Barclay, who
was to become the apologist or chief arguer in defense
of Quaker thought.

If the new generation was less aggressive, less restless, less ready to travel afar for their truth, George of
necessity was, too. He was no longer able to go long
nights without sleep and days without food. He had
too many painful reminders of his imprisonment—ach-
ing joints, arthritic bones. When Fox came out of Scarborough prison in 1666, he saw how the widespread
Friends needed a re-ordering of their priorities, and a
tighter organization. Accordingly, Fox went about for
the next four years tending to the *business* of the
Friends.

George began by setting up regular meetings
throughout England. These *Monthly Meetings,* as they
were realistically if not poetically named, were for
business, not worship. Still, they had this in common
with the meetings for worship: no one person set himself above the others in deciding what business was to
be considered or acted upon. All Friends made the decision together. As Fox wrote: "Friends are not to meet
like a company of people about town or parish business
. . . but to wait upon the Lord." Monthly Meetings

were the first real beginning of the *Society of Friends,* as the Quakers are still called today.* The first business meeting had already been established in 1654, the first General Meeting in 1658. But before 1666, there was no regular system of meetings. It was to the perfection of such a system that George turned upon his release from Scarborough.

The system that Fox devised was marked by a simplicity of structure and method. There were no hierarchies of officials, no sacraments, no paraphernalia. As Rufus Jones has remarked, "One might have supposed that chaos would have resulted . . . but it did not." The system of meetings was able to deal with the day-to-day problems of social injustice, poverty, education, and prison reform in a practical way.

The perfecting of this system of monthly meetings (and thence quarterly and yearly meetings) and the structuring of the Society remained Fox's task for the rest of his life. It did not mean an end to his traveling, nor unfortunately, to his stay in jails. He was still "in journeys often . . . in prison more frequent." But the governing of the now vast network of local meetings, the welding together, making unified, the diverse Quakers, was to occupy George's mind for the next twenty-four years.

"Organizing" sounds like such a dull, dry task, but it encompassed more than mere paper work. And some of the ideas that early Quakers experimented with still

* The actual term "Society of Friends" did not come into common usage until the 1800s.

remain models of modern thinking. Fox suggested that the local meetings set up apprenticeship programs, especially for children of the poor. (Think of our modern Job Corps.) Friends schools were started on the principle of "teaching everything civil and useful in creation." (Think of our modern "open-school" systems.) Meetings for Suffering were set up, to assure that Friends in prison would not have to worry about their families and that they would be in touch with the outside world. (Modern prison reform emphasizes the need for family visits, and the need to see that the prisoner's family is well provided for.)

By 1669, though, Fox was getting restless again. He was feeling better, the horrors of prison had receded. He determined to go to Ireland to preach in the old way.

On the surface, Ireland seems a rather poor choice for a Protestant missionary. The South was Catholic, and violently opposed to both Protestants and Englishmen, since Cromwell had left a bad taste for both in Irish mouths. And even in the Protestant North there was a language barrier. Most Irishmen spoke Celtic. George did not. (This was a small point as far as Fox was concerned. One of his minor vanities was his presumed knowledge of many tongues, though it is not certain that he knew more than a few words in any language other than English.)

Once in Ireland, however, surrounded by Irish Quakers who could speak the language, Fox had a relatively calm journey. And when he sailed home from

Ireland, the Irish Quakers followed in their boats till Fox's ship was "near a league at sea, their love drawing them, though not without danger." George was impressed with the few Irish Friends he met, and he wrote that they were "a good, weighty, and true people . . . [with] an excellent spirit in them, worthy to be visited."

Fox landed at Bristol and hearing that Margaret Fell was there visiting her daughter and son-in-law, Isabel and William Yeamans, he hurried to join her. The year 1669 was not just a time for journeying to Ireland. It was a time for Fox's journey into marriage as well.

"I had seen from the Lord a considerable time before," Fox wrote in his *Journal*, "that I should take Margaret Fell to be my wife." It was a strange understatement, for nowhere else had Fox even discussed this in print. He was forty-five, Margaret was fifty-five. It was evidently a step they had talked about privately before, waiting until the time was right—and they were both out of prison.

The marriage of George Fox and Margaret Fell was more than a simple wedding. It was a symbolic act as well, marrying as it did the "Father" of Quakerism with the "Nursing Mother." So it was doubly important that, though they had both thought a great deal about such a step, they should consult others, too. Accordingly, Margaret first called her children together and asked in a family council if they had any feelings for or against such a marriage. Her daughters and

their husbands, all good Quakers, already called Fox
"Father," and were unanimous in their approval. Only
George Fell, the one son, who neither admired Fox nor
was a Friend, disapproved. But for reasons of his own,
reasons which soon became apparent, he did not stand
in the way of the wedding.

Next, George and Margaret announced their inten-
tions to Friends in general. William Penn was to write
later that their marriage was "God's word of life."

Still, George was not completely satisfied. He
wanted to be sure that none of the inheritance of Judge
Fell's children would be forfeited in any way by the
marriage. He was so persistent that Margaret finally
told him to stop talking about it.

Fox's answer was typical. "I am a plain man and
would have things done plainly, for I seek not any outward advantage to myself."

The last thing that Margaret Fell did before she
married Fox was to transfer Swarthmore Hall to her
daughters, who promised to keep it open for the Quakers. She did this because, by the terms of the judge's
will, she would have to give up the house if she remar-
ried.

It was this act that infuriated her son George. He
had assumed that Swarthmore Hall would automatically come to him. He wanted the manor house for
himself, and he started to scheme with Kirkby and
other Quaker-haters how to get it.

George and Margaret knew nothing of her son's
plans when they gathered the family and some ninety-

four Friends for the simple wedding ceremony that took place October 27, 1669, at the Broad-Mead Meetinghouse in Bristol.

A Quaker wedding is not like the usual marriage ceremony, just as a Quaker Meeting is not like the usual church service. There is no priest or minister officiating. The man and woman marry themselves before God. That is, they stand up and pledge themselves to one another in the sight of God and the Friends. A certificate is signed by those in attendance, and taken as soon as possible to a Justice of the Peace.

Margaret and George were not the first Quakers to be married in this manner. For years there had been a struggle to have Friends' marriages considered legal. Margaret Fox had been in the forefront of this fight, which had been won only in 1661, when Quaker weddings were recognized by law.

About the time of his marriage, Fox first met William Penn, a recent convert to Quakerism. The 23-year-old Londoner was the son of a wealthy father who had just arrived from Ireland. It was an association that would grow warmer and closer with the years and their mutual travels in America.

Penn, though quarreling with his father because of the Quakers, still had access to the royal court. He became the official pleader for Quaker causes among the nobility the way Fox had been with Cromwell. Being a member of the court also gave Penn access to its land grants. He had heard of the fertile lands north of Catholic Maryland in America. It was an area which was still undeveloped. The Indians were reputed to be friendly. It seemed the perfect place for a Quaker settlement. Penn wanted Fox's approval for his immigration scheme. Although nothing came of their first tentative talks except friendship, it was the start of what would finally become Pennsylvania.

George and Margaret Fox had a one-week honeymoon in Bristol. Then they traveled back to Oldstone where they parted, George to continue his work of organizing, Margaret to run Swarthmore Hall. They were not to see each other again for four years. Only their letters, filled with love and understanding, kept them in touch.

Margaret had barely gotten home when she was "haled out of her house to Lancaster prison again, by an order obtained from King and council, to fetch her back to prison upon the old *praemunire*." It was George Fell's work. The idle, extravagant son had forced his own mother's arrest. He had petitioned the king for his mother's share of the inheritance, including Swarthmore Hall—though technically it now belonged to the Fell daughters—and the king had granted his petition. Young Fell sent word that he intended to reclaim Swarthmore Hall after his mother was in jail. When she heard that, his sister Mary hurried home to remove as much from the house as she could. But she needn't have hurried. Inexplicably, young George Fell died the next year, October 1670. "Cut off," Fox might have said, while his mother lay in Lancaster prison.

Margaret was not the only Quaker to be imprisoned

in 1670. Under pressure from the Jesuits, and with a
Catholic uprising feared in every clandestine meeting,
King Charles and his council renewed the Conventicle
Act in May. Not only were meetings of more than five
people illegal, but the renewed Act made house owners
where such meetings were held liable to imprisonment
as well. There was a high incentive to be paid to in-
formers. Most damaging of all, it would now take only
one judge—and not a number of judges together—to
convict a person under the new law.

The results were that Quakers in unprecedented
numbers were torn from meetings and thrown into jail.
The Act was against all the Nonconformist Sects, but
the Quakers were the only ones who continued to meet
openly. It was said that the Nonconformists would, in
their secret night meetings, pray to God to keep the
Quakers steadfast. They even thanked God "that He
had enabled the Quakers to stand in the gap and bear
the brunt and keep the blow off them," according to
Whitehead.

Margaret's daughters had managed to get an order
from the king for her discharge, but because of the renewed Conventicle Act, the authorities found excuse
after excuse to keep her in prison for almost a year
after the king's order.

While Margaret was in prison, George felt he had to
test the new Act. Never one to fly from the eye of the
storm, George decided to disobey the law on the first
Sunday it was announced, and to disobey it flagrantly.
So he chose to go to Gracechurch Street Meeting

House in London (he called it *Gracious Street*) where he "expected the storm was most to begin."

The authorities, feeling the same way, had already posted guards at the front and back entrances of the Meeting House to keep Friends out of the building. The Quakers were milling about the courtyard, listening to a speaker when George arrived. As soon as the Friend finished speaking and stepped down, George began to preach. He spoke of the persecutions and how the Quakers were a peaceable people, loving even those who persecuted them. Just as he reached the line "Blessed are the peacemakers," some burly soldiers reached up and pulled him down from the bench where he was standing. They dragged him off to be questioned. As he was pulled through the streets, George heard the people call out, "Have a care of him, he is a princely man."

After several hours of questioning George and two companions who had been arrested with him were released.

"Wither wilt thou go?" asked one of the Friends to George.

"To Gracechurch Street Meeting again," was his instant reply.

By then, of course, the meeting was over. But Fox had come mainly to show his contempt for a law that would have denied a meeting, as George put it, of the twelve apostles. He also wanted to find out what had happened after his arrest. He learned that "As fast as some that were speaking were taken down [by the arresting soldiers] others were moved of the Lord to stand up and speak."

Despite his vigor in the face of this and other dangers, the increasing persecutions and his years in prison were telling on George. He was worried about Margaret and the other imprisoned Quakers throughout the country. He began to have a re-occurrence of the nervous troubles that had plagued him at the time of James Nayler's release. In his own words, he felt "burthened with the world's spirits," and these burdens manifested themselves physically. He had trouble eating and sleeping. He lost his sight and hearing, though typically he made light of it, saying that it was a sign for those who would not see or hear the truth. At last he lay in a coma for days. The rumor soon got about that Fox had died.

However, without warning, Fox suddenly awoke from his coma and sat up in bed. He ordered his clothes brought. He had heard, while in the coma, that another Friend was ill and he wanted to comfort the man. Gerrard Roberts, the sick Friend, lived some twelve miles into the country. It didn't matter that George was much sicker than Friend Roberts. He insisted that he had to visit the man. After having been all but carried down the stairs to the carriage, Fox rode sitting up all the way there. As they traveled, Fox began to see again. At first he could only make out the fields, then people in the fields.

George stayed three weeks with Friend Roberts before he set out again to visit another Friend who was dying. Even in the hours of his own near-fatal illness, Fox had time for others.

By the Spring of 1671, Fox had recovered sufficiently from his "death" to send letters to those suffering in prisons. Since he was still too ill to walk among his Friends, he took his pen as his walking stick, and wrote:

My Dear Friends:

The Seed is above all. In it walk; in which ye all have life.

Be not amazed at the weather; for always the just suffered by the unjust, but the just had the dominion.

All along ye may see, by faith the mountains were subdued; and the rage of the wicked, with his fiery darts, was quenched. Though the waves and storms be high, yet your faith will keep you, so as to swim above them; for they are but for a time, and the Truth is without time. Therefore keep on the mountain of holiness, ye who are led to it by the Light.

Do not think that anything will outlast the Truth. For the Truth standeth sure; and is over that which is out of the Truth. For the good will overcome the evil; the light, darkness; the life, death; virtue, vice; and righteousness, unrighteousness. The false prophet cannot overcome the true; but the true prophet, Christ, will overcome all the false.

So be faithful, and live in that which doth not think the time long.

G.F.

The "burthens" which had afflicted Fox's spirits and led to his sickness eventually slackened of their own accord. The persecutors were becoming tired of their bloody game, especially with such peaceable victims. As the persecutions of the Quakers ceased, so did Fox's physical reaction to them, and he was able to function normally again.

One of the first things he did was to send two women Friends (one of them Hannah Stranger, Nayler's old follower) to the king to remind him that Margaret Fox still remained in prison. King Charles signed a personal discharge that released Margaret both from jail and from the old *praemunire,* which she had been under for almost seven years.

At the same time, George wrote to Margaret telling her she would soon be released and asking her to hurry to London to say good-bye to him. Now that he was well again, Fox had decided to go to America.

[America] where things were much
out of order.
—GEORGE FOX, *Journal*

Chapter 15

America

The idea of going to America was not a new one for
the Quakers. Friends had already died there for their
faith. But it was the first time George Fox had sailed to
the New World. It would be two years before he returned.

Margaret Fox was released from prison just in time
to say good-bye to her husband. It seemed they were
always meeting to part, but as she wrote, "we were
very willing both of us to live apart for some years on
God's account."

Margaret joined the ship's company of the yacht *Industry* for a single night as it sailed to the mouth of the
harbor. When she left it in the morning, she left

George and twelve Friends with fifty other passengers ready to sail to America.

The company of Friends consisted of eleven men and two women, one being the same Elizabeth Hooton that Fox had first converted in 1646. She was now sixty-nine years old.

It was early in the morning of August 12, 1671, when the two-masted yacht set sail. She was a swift ship but unfortunately, as her passengers were soon to discover, not very seaworthy. She leaked so much that both sailors and passengers had to take turns manning the pumps.

The ship was about three weeks out to sea on a bright, calm afternoon when the lookout spied a strange ship about four leagues astern.

"A Sallee man-o'-war," he called down.

The words ran quickly through the ship. Sallee, a seagoing port in Morocco, lent its name to the ships in which the Moorish pirates sailed. The *Industry* was being chased by buccaneers.

Captain Thomas Forster tried to soothe the agitated passengers. "Come let us go to supper," he said calmly. "And when it grows dark we shall lose him."

The captain's manner relieved no one but the thirteen Friends whose faith was so strong they literally cast out fear.

As the sun went down, however, George peered out of his cabin's porthole and discovered that the pirate ship was gaining. Each time the *Industry* changed her course, the Moorish ship altered its course, too. It was only a matter of hours before they would be overtaken.

Apparently, Captain Forster felt this way, too. Although he did not admit it to the other passengers, the captain was extremely worried and told Fox so. He had come into George's cabin at dark to ask for advice.

"I am no mariner," replied Fox, stating the obvious. "Do what thee thinks best to do."

The captain answered that there were only two possibilities: to outrun the pirates or to take a tacking course, as they were now doing, and evade them.

Fox was quiet for a moment. Then he said that if these were indeed pirates, tacking would not work. Outrunning the fast Sallee also appeared impossible in their leaky condition.

But Forster and his men pressed George for some kind of answer. It seems odd that they should have wanted his advice, he being neither sailor nor fighter. Yet his calm, resolute manner impressed them. They knew his reputation as a religious man and had also heard of his "magic." They hoped he might intercede with God for them—or at least save them with magic. As they said to Fox, "if the mariners had taken [Saint] Paul's counsel, they had not come to the damage they did."

Fox did more than intercede for the ship. He took direct action, though it was, he insisted, God-inspired action. First, he explained, that this was a trial of faith and he would have to meditate until God spoke directly to him. After a few minutes in which the captain and his men stood in reverent silence, Fox said he had a plan.

He ordered that all the candles but the one they steered by be extinguished so that the pirates would have no light by which to track the *Industry*. The passengers were to be absolutely still. By this time, it was eleven o'clock. The dark was heavy and only a partial moon was out, quickly hidden by the many clouds. In the dark, by the light of a single candle, the *Industry* resumed tacking. Suddenly, a fresh gale sprang up and, as Fox says, "the Lord hid us from them; we sailed briskly on and saw them no more."

Almost two months passed on board ship before the *Industry* made its first stop in the New World. The leaky vessel finally sailed into the harbor at Barbados.

The trip at sea had done nothing to help Fox's already weakened health. When they landed, he collapsed for several weeks at the home of Friend Richard Forstall. He had rheumatic fever. Since he could not move about and preach, he dictated letters and wrote papers which were printed in England.

News of Fox's condition spread quickly to the communities of Friends awaiting his arrival. They gathered instead at Forstall's house for meetings there, so they could be with George and benefit from his mature advice. His advice was especially valuable for these new communities. He could deal with their spiritual problems out of a knowledge of a lifetime's service to God.

It was while he was abed in Forstall's house that he

first met and dealt with the problem of Negro slavery, a concern that was to be in the forefront of Quaker thought in the centuries to come.* George was aware of the problems of slave and master, for a number of Friends were slaves in the Arabic countries, either captured by pirates and shipped there, or taken when they came as missionaries. "I desired them," wrote Fox about slave owners, "that they would cause their overseers to deal mildly and gently with their negroes, and not use cruelty towards them, as the manner of some hath been and is; and that after certain years of servitude, they would make them free."

For the seventeenth century, this was an enlightened and humanistic view. Fox would later call slavery a great cruelty and point out that slaves, too, possessed the Inner Light, a view not held by those who considered black men animals.

After three months in the Barbados, much of it sick in bed, Fox felt it was time to move on. His first small trip was to Jamaica, where he sailed with most of his English company. Several stayed behind to consolidate the work done in the Barbados. A week after they landed, Elizabeth Hooton died. The first woman to be a minister in the Quaker movement, she had suffered uncounted tortures and imprisonment in the cause of religious freedom. She had just turned seventy.

The shrunken company of English Friends finally

* In 1776, the Quakers petitioned the Continental Congress to end slavery, and decided to exclude from the Society of Friends any Quakers who held slaves.

set sail for the American mainland. Despite contrary winds and heavy storms, they made it to Patuxent River bay in Maryland in six and a half weeks.

So it was that on June 28, 1672, the first real work in America was begun. The Quaker company divided themselves into several "coasts"; two went on to lay the groundwork for Fox's visit in New England, four to Virginia, and Fox and four others, plus a company of American Friends, went by boat to the Eastern shore of Chesapeake Bay.

What Fox had in mind was not a mission to convert the unconverted, though there was always a chance of that. Rather he came to organize the American meetings along the lines of the English system. He considered the Quakers in America "much out of order." He wanted to unify the scattered groups, show them how to keep records of births, marriages, deaths. He was also there to smooth out differences, to bring back into the mainstream those meetings or individuals who, like James Nayler, had gone too far astray.

Fox's first meetings were so successful that he had Friends, non-Friends, and even large companies of Indians attending them. Fox, who knew very little about Indians, described them as "the Indian emperor and his kings . . . with their cockarooses," or chiefs.

The Friends with George began their long and often tedious journey towards New England. It was to take them through woods and wildernesses, over bogs and swamps. It would mean nights camping in the woods or sleeping in an Indian's wigwam, long rides on horse-

back soaked by the rains and chilled by the early
spring winds. It was not an easy trip even for a young
man in the best of health, but George, now in his late
forties, ill from years of imprisonment and persecution,
managed as well as any backwoodsman.

At last reaching Long Island, Fox met with a large
community of Friends. They were having a four-day
meeting. This was one of the communities that needed
George's special touch. There were "bad spirits"
among them: contentious, prejudiced folk who were
dividing the Long Island Friends into several warring
factions. Weary from weeks of travel, Fox still took
time to have special meetings with these "discontented
people." George wrote: "We had a day of washing and
sweeping. . . ." Through a combination of will power
and God power, he was able to expose the "bad spirits"
for what they were and so save the meeting from fall-
ing apart.

From Long Island, the Quakers went by boat to
Rhode Island where Fox was extremely impressed with
the colony's freedom of worship. This freedom was
manifested in the diligent attention paid to speakers
during a marathon six-day meeting the Friends held
when they arrived. Fox said he had never seen its like.

In Rhode Island, even governor Nicholas Easton
was a Friend. His new wife, Ann Clayton, had once
been a maid at Swarthmore Hall and she greeted
George with true affection. Fox advised the governor
on state matters as well as spiritual ones.

The only trouble George had in Rhode Island was

with its founder, Roger Williams. It is ironic that Williams, known for his belief in freedom of thought, did not like George personally. He even published a book against Fox bearing the humorous title *George Fox digged out of his Burrows.*

Many non-Friends attended the Quaker meetings in Rhode Island, and some magistrates were overheard to say that if they could raise the money, they would like to hire Fox as a regular minister. Fox shook his head ruefully when he was told this. It was obvious that these men did not understand the Quaker message that *each man is his own minister.* Such statements made George leave Rhode Island, "for if their eye were so much on me, or on any of us, [the Rhode Islanders] would not come to their own Teacher." He meant, of course, "to bring every one to his own Teacher *in* himself."

George gathered his companions and they left for Shelter Island, a small bit of land at the eastern tip of Long Island where Nathaniel Sylvester had created a haven for the persecuted New England Friends. From Shelter Island, the Quakers set off for a long tour of public preaching. They traveled through what is now lower New York State, New Jersey, Pennsylvania, Delaware, Maryland, Virginia, and the Carolinas. Fox never visited the large New England communities of Friends in Massachusetts or New Hampshire. It may be that he felt they did not need his special gifts.

In Maryland, the meetings were so large that about 1,000 people at a time crowded in. Even the newly-enlarged Meeting House in Baltimore could not contain them.

Through Virginia and the Carolinas, the weather and the roads conspired to try to defeat the Quaker travelers. As Fox described it: "much of it [was] plashy, and pretty full of great bogs and swamps, so that we were commonly wet to the knees and lay abroad at nights in the woods by a fire."

The governor of Virginia, like the governor of Rhode Island, received the English Friends with great kindness. However, one of his guests, a doctor, set upon the Quakers and disagreed violently that there was that of God in every man. He was especially enraged with the idea that there was any of God in the Indians. It was a typical Puritan view.

The Quakers, of course, thought differently. They believed in the universality of the Inner Light. "Every man was enlightened by the divine light of Christ, and I saw it shine through all," said Fox.

The Friends believed that Indians, Negroes, Muslims, Jews, or any of the Christian sects had the Seed of God in them. As Isaac Penington put it, "It is not the outward name but the inward life and power which is the Saviour."

Furthermore, the Quakers felt that since this Light was universal, it was the duty of every Friend to "answer" that of God in everyone; that is, to develop or stimulate or call forth that of God in other people. This idea of "answering that of God in everyone" is the basis of the Quakers' theory of social behavior and it permeates their every action.

At the Virginia governor's house, in order to answer the doctor's vehement argument, Fox called over an Indian to speak to them. He asked, "When thou liest or do wrong to any one, is there not something in thee that reprovest thee for it?" The Indian assured him that this was so, and that he was certainly ashamed if he had done or said anything wrong. That, George exclaimed to the doctor, was the Inner Light. This so confounded the doctor that he began to disown any Scripture that might teach such a doctrine, and so defeated his argument in everyone's eyes.

Fox's entire American journey took two years. Though there were no really spectacular arrests or confrontations, the entire trip was considered a success by all. Fox had gotten to see the colonials; they had gotten to see him. The message of organization had been carried to the hinterlands. And later on, when George was to meet again with William Penn, Fox's broad knowledge of the temper of the American people and the condition of the land played an important role in choosing the place for the great Quaker colony, the "Holy Experiment" on the western shore of the Delaware River.

Fox and a good many of his original band set sail for England on the *Society of Bristol* in the spring of 1673. Despite "foul weather and contrary winds," it took only five weeks to get to the British port of Bristol. They landed on June 20, 1673.

Women as well as men, might know, possess,
perform, and discharge their offices and services
in the house of God.

—GEORGE FOX, *Journal*

Chapter 16

Schism

Dear Heart:

*This day we came into Bristol, near night, from the sea;
glory to the Lord God over all for ever, who was our convoy,
and steered our course! who is the God of the whole earth, of
the seas and winds, and made the clouds His chariots, beyond
all words, blessed be His name for ever! He is over all in His
great power and wisdom. Amen. Robert Widders and James
Lancaster are with me, and we are well; glory to the Lord
forever, who hath carried us through many perils, perils by
water and in storms, perils by pirates and robbers, perils in
the wilderness and amongst false professors. Praises to Him
whose glory is over all for ever, Amen. Therefore mind the
fresh life, and live all to God in it. I do intend (if the Lord*

will) to stay a while this-away; it may be till the fair. So no more, but my love to all Friends.

G.F.

Bristol, the 28th Day of the 4th Month, 1673.*

As soon as she received this letter, Margaret Fox hurried south to Bristol with two of her daughters and her son-in-law Thomas Lower to meet George. Others, such as William Penn and his new wife, were also rushing to Bristol to greet him. They celebrated his safe return with a number of large meetings at the Bristol fair.

Slowly this large company of Quakers journeyed towards London which was one of the centers of Quaker activity. Along the way, they held meetings and preached to large crowds, quite in contempt of the still-enforced Conventicle Act.

They turned northwards at last to go to Fenny Drayton, where George planned to visit his dying mother before returning for a much-needed rest at Swarthmore Hall.

At supper one evening not far from Worcester, Fox had a presentiment that he would shortly be arrested and jailed. He said nothing of this to Margaret, her daughters, or Lower. After so long a separation, he did not want to spoil the home-coming. But the very next day his presentiment came true.

George and Lower were sitting and talking after a large meeting when a local justice and an informer-

---

* The calendar today is two months different.

priest arrested them. Ostensibly, Fox and Lower were arrested for violating the Conventicle Act. However, because the priest had been delayed at a christening (he "stayed for the sprinkling" said George), the judge and informer were too late to catch the two Quakers at the actual meeting. Technically, therefore, there were no grounds for arrest. According to the Conventicle Act, arrests had to be made *during* the meeting. It mattered little. Fox and Lower were taken to Worcester jail. Margaret and her daughters were sent on to Swarthmore Hall in the company of other Friends.

At the Worcester jail, George and Lower were held over a month awaiting trial. While they were in prison, Lower wrote to influential friends at court.

Because of those friends, the trial itself was held in unusually civil conditions. But it did not change the outcome, for this trial was a simple replay of all Fox's trials in the past. Having no case against the two men, the presiding judge dragged out the Oath of Allegiance. When Fox refused to swear, he was led back to jail.

As soon as George was out of the courtroom, the judges leaned over and informed Lower he was free to go.

Lower asked why, since they had both been taken together on the same charge, he was at liberty and Fox jailed. It is a question that still echoes in courtrooms today when men and women are sentenced unequally in cases of conscience.

The judges answered, "You may be gone about your

business, for we have nothing more to say to you."

At that, the court was dismissed and the judges left the hall. But Lower pursued them right into their chambers.

The Chief Justice turned to young Lower in a fury. "If you be not content, we will tender you the oaths also, and send you to your father."

Lower informed the judges that they might do as they saw fit, but that he would go to prison by himself and wait upon his father there.

Justice Parker, the man who had arrested Lower originally, turned angrily on him. "Do you not think that I had not cause to send your father and you to prison when you had so great a meeting that the parson of the parish complained to me that he hath lost the greater part of his parishioners?"

Lower was not impressed. He said quietly, "I have heard that the priest of that parish comes so seldom to visit his flock (but once, it may be or twice a year, to gather up his tithes) that it was but charity in my father to visit such a forlorn and forsaken flock."

To Lower's surprise, the judges burst out laughing. He soon realized that the priest he was talking about, Joseph Crowther, was there in the room. Lower was smart enough not to apologize for his words but to let the truth stand.

Lower was not thrown into prison, yet he was as good as his word. He stayed in jail the entire time Fox was there, attending to Fox's needs and tending the

older man when he became sick. Many of George's old
illnesses returned in prison, so Lower's constant presence was a blessing. Even though this prison was much
better than any of his former ones, and the jailers so
lenient that they even left him in the charge of an 11-
year-old boy, Fox's recurring arthritis and stomach ul-
cers gave him no rest. He had a vision of himself
"amongst the graves and dead corpses."

While Fox was in prison, word came that his aged
mother had died. George's last imprisonment had been
her death blow. Though it had been many years since
Fox had even seen his parents (his father had died
some years previously), Fox wrote of Mary Fox that "I
did in verity love her as ever one could a mother."

During this long imprisonment, Margaret Fox traveled several times to see her husband. On one of her
trips, in October 1674, she went on to London and
spoke to the king, telling him of the farcical trial and
the way the oath was used as a snare for Quakers.
King Charles was willing to give Fox a royal pardon
and Margaret quickly sent the news to Worcester
prison.

But Fox would have none of it. To him, a pardon
implied that the king was willing to forgive him for
any wrongs he had done. George knew he had done no
wrong, and so needed no pardon. "I would rather have
lain in prison all my days," he told Margaret, "than
have come out in any way dishonourable to Truth."
What George wanted was a retrial, to be cleared of
any wrongdoing before a judge. He was absolutely in-

capable of taking the easy way out in matters of conscience.

Lower and Margaret managed to retain the services of a fine Welsh lawyer, Thomas Corbett, and they set the wheels of justice in motion again. Fox was to be retried in London in April 1675. Everyone recognized that the original trial had been a farce, even the magistrates. To underline this, they made Lower a deputy and commissioned him to bring Fox to London for the trial. The two Quakers made their slow way—Fox was too ill to travel quickly—to London, preaching and attending large meetings as they went.

Corbett was an excellent lawyer and based his argument on the fact that *praemunire* was not a legal reason for imprisonment but merely a summons for trial. The judges agreed that the original trial had been full of errors. At least, that was the reason they gave out. Personally, they felt that the entire thing had been a private vendetta against Fox. The new judges ordered George freed. He had been in jail fourteen months.

Fox was now to enter upon the third period of his active life. In his youth, he had been a roving evangelist, preaching and converting the mystical professors to his truth. In middle age, he had been an administrator and organizer, welding those same mystical professors into a single Society of Friends. In his old age and ill health, he was to become the elder statesman, mending breaches with his tongue and pen.

At the time of Fox's release from jail, a certain Lord

Berkley was going bankrupt. He was the nobleman who owned part of the province of New Jersey in which the Quakers were interested. He was ready to sell his American lands. Fox and Penn together worked for the purchase of the land—1,000 pounds for 4,000 square miles of New Jersey land. Penn turned his energies completely towards the colonization of the New World.

But Fox could not. During his imprisonment, a new schism—a division in the Quaker movement—had come to a head. It was one which George had first tried to deal with on his return from America. It was the third such trial to threaten the Friends. The first had been Nayler's fall. The second had been the "hat controversy." Friend John Perrot returned from Rome with a mystical command from his Inner Light that he must keep his hat on, even in prayer. This had triggered a small schism in 1661. From Perrot's hat to anarchy was but a short step. Perrot's followers began to denounce any human arrangements, including setting a specific time for meeting. But the third schism, the one the newly-returned Fox had come upon in 1673, was to be the worst.

Friends John Story and John Wilkinson, who had been among the First Publishers of Truth, were the instigators. They had begun by denouncing the Quaker practice of women's meetings. Using St. Paul to bolster their arguments, Story and Wilkinson declared that women should hold a lesser, subservient position in the Society of Friends. Fox, an ardent upholder of women's

rights from his earliest ministry, was unalterably opposed to their view.

At their first confrontation, Fox had answered Story
and Wilkinson simply. "Women as well as men, might
know, possess, perform, and discharge their offices and
services in the house of God."

Perhaps if George had not been imprisoned soon
after this first confrontation, that might have been the
last of the Wilkinson–Story schism. But while Fox
served his final term in Worcester jail, the first small
rumblings became louder. By the time Fox was out of
jail again, the Wilkinson–Story controversy was ready
to split the Friends in two. George had to act. Even a
trip to Holland and Germany, quiet and without real
incident, was secondary to dealing with the schism that
was rapidly dividing the Quaker ranks.

At first Wilkinson and Story had been content to
rage against the place of women in the Society. But
since they couched their argument against women in
terms of "personal revelation," the argument grew.
They said that it had been personally revealed to them
that women did not deserve a high place in the Friends
movement. When Fox argued against this denuncia-
tion of women ministers and women leaders, they accused him of being against personal revelation, against
the Inner Light.

It was the same story that had been played out in
both the Nayler and the Perrot hat controversies. Did
Fox have the right to encourage the subjugation of personal revelation to that of the group? George and his

followers said yes. Wilkinson and Story said no. Fox
felt that authority had to rest only with the group as a
whole. But the "troublesome spirits" in the Wilkinson–
Story camp were against any settled system of group
government. To them, the yearly meetings and the
regular business meetings were just a regular church in
another form.

While Fox was trying to set up a system to keep the
Quaker movement going with or without the strong
personalities of certain Quaker preachers, the schism-
makers were crying for anarchy. In a way, the Wilkinson–Story people had an important point. There are
dangers in too much organization as well as too little.
Too often, the bones of a system replace its spirit. A
balance had to be struck.

But a balance had already been struck in the
Quaker movement. There were no definite spiritual
superiors like priests, but rather loving counselors.
These counselors did not lay down infallible guidelines
or decisions. Instead, there were "suggestions" drawn
up by various Quakers. As one of them wrote, "These
things we do not lay upon you as a rule or form to walk
by, but that all with the measure of light which is pure
and holy may be guided."

Fox's way of dealing with the Wilkinson–Story
schism that threatened the fabric of the Society was
twofold. First, sick as he was, he traveled to as many of
the disturbed meetings as possible, personally arguing
with the malcontents. Secondly, he used his pen both
as a weapon and as a welder.

Towards the end of 1675, Thomas Lower and he settled for a while in Swarthmore Hall. It was the first
time in thirty-two years that he was living in his own
home. It was the first real rest outside of prison that he
had allowed himself since he started his ministry as a
youth. George Fox was fifty-one years old, and very
tired. He spent the next two years setting his papers in
order.

Together, Lower and George worked on Fox's *Journal,* considered today one of the masterpieces of spiritual autobiography. It was not only an autobiography,
however; it was also a work about the origins and history of the Quaker movement. Fox's *Journal* radiates
sincerity, honesty, and faith; it shows Fox's independ-
ence, directness of action and speech; it hints at the
power of the man. Though much of its grammar was
tidied up by Lower and thirteen subsequent editors,
the raw, rustic, charismatic preacher comes through. It
would be published in 1694, three years after Fox's
death. Not only the *Journal* has been published, but
also his hundreds of letters—*Epistles,* as they were
called. These are a living testament to his energy.

While he was at Swarthmore Hall working on his
papers and *Journal,* Fox heard that there were still
Friends trying to mend the Wilkinson–Story breach.
But Fox would brook no compromises. He was realistic
enough to know that certain divisive issues, like Wilkinson–Story, could break the Quakers. So he took deci-
sive, sure steps to keep the movement together. He
wrote in 1677: "They that are so keen for John Story

and John Wilkinson, let them take them, and the separation. . . . Do not strive, nor make bargains with that which is out of Truth." Fox preferred amputation to the spreading of the Wilkinson–Story infection to the entire body of Friends.

It was a sorry time for the Friends. The Wilkinson–Story party separated themselves from the main body of Quakers in 1678. They were opposed to any authority exercised by the group over the individual.

As a result, the anarchistic Wilkinson–Story movement died out within the century, though many of the questions the schism raised are still being answered. Fox's organization—and the Quaker spirit of unity in the Inner Light that it embodied—remains to this day.

All is well; the Seed of God
reigns over all and over death itself.
     —GEORGE FOX, AS REPORTED
     by WILLIAM PENN

Chapter 17

Death and Transfiguration

The next few years found George Fox growing steadily
weaker and slower. Yet throughout this last long de-
scent towards death, he kept busy writing documents,
letters, articles, and working on his journal. Until his
final illness, he was concerned with others, spending
his remaining strength like a prodigal, helping Parliament draft legislation on freedom of religion, writing
letters of encouragement to the suffering Irish Friends,
working to set up the "Holy Experiment" in America,
and always appealing for unity within the Society of
Friends.

Things in England had taken a decided change,
though whether for better or worse, it was hard to say.

In 1684, only a few days after Margaret Fox had pleaded in vain for some relief for the persecuted Friends, Charles II died. His brother James, an ardent Catholic, assumed the throne, but not without bitter opposition from the Protestants. The following year, Charles's popular illegitimate son, the Duke of Monmouth, landed in the western part of England with a small force to stir up a rebellion that would place him, a Protestant, on the throne. Monmouth was defeated at Sedgemoor by John Churchill, the illustrious ancestor of Winston Churchill. The Duke, a dashing if weak-willed figure, was executed and thus ended the Protestant rebellion for several years.

James was a strong-minded king on one subject, and that was Catholicism. He tried to pack Parliament and his councils with men of his own religion. His dead brother Charles had been a secret Catholic, converting only on his deathbed. But he had ruled England as though he were a Protestant. James would have none of this.

Ironically, some of the new king's measures to relieve Catholic suffering aided the Quakers. Unlike Cromwell and Charles, who both had grudging admiration for the Friends, James had written, "I have no great reason to be well satisfied with Quakers in general." Indeed, with their emphasis on personal revelation and the ministry of each man, not to mention their abhorrence of rigid church services, the Quakers were utterly opposed to Catholicism—and James knew it.

However, on May 16, 1685, James released all *prae-munired* Quakers who were in jail for refusing to swear the oath of allegiance. Hundreds of Quakers were set free when James affixed his signature to the eleven skins of vellum with the great seal attached. This royal order was carried from prison to prison where Friends were confined. The jailers had to search through the eleven skins on which some 491 names were written (including a few non-Quakers like John Bunyan, author of *Pilgrim's Progress*) to find their own prisoners.

The excitement with which the freed Quakers were met set all England ablaze. George and Margaret Fox went to meeting after meeting to join in the thanksgiving, but they did not go together. George was in London once again, Margaret at Swarthmore Hall.

It seems strange now that such a marriage could have been considered successful. In the twelve years of Margaret and George's marriage, they were to be together less than four years. But Margaret was as committed to the establishment of Quakerism as was George. She realized that, even though imprisonment or travels kept them apart, they were, in George's words, "united in the Seed."

While Fox was working in London, Margaret kept the Quaker center at Swarthmore Hall open. She did this despite growing pressure from her old enemy Colonel Kirkby. He even said he would stop at nothing short of murder to persecute the Fells. "Whilst you have anything," he told her, "we will take it." Yet she won in the end. Margaret Fox lived to be eighty-eight, grandmother to thirty-two Quaker children, an out-spoken elder stateswoman of the Quaker movement who even wrote a book defending the rights of women to preach.

Catholic James was on the throne only three turbu-lent years when he was forced to flee because of Protes-tant pressure. His daughter Mary and her Dutch hus-band William of Orange, both good Protestants, took the throne of England and ruled it jointly.

William and Mary issued the Toleration Act the fol-lowing year, 1689. It was a grudging act that said dis-senters could hold meetings as long as the doors to the meeting halls were not fastened. Meeting in "secret," in other words, was still frowned upon. While it did not actually remove the old laws from the books, the Tol-eration Act made sure that there would be no penalty for breaking those laws. This did not totally wipe out religious persecution, but it did go a long way towards it. In fact it went so far, many Quakers felt disinclined to risk anything more for religious freedom. They merely sat back and thanked God for what they had already achieved.

But not George Fox. Sick and aged beyond his sixty-five years, Fox kept busy writing and preaching until the very end.

The end came in 1691. On January 11, a Sunday, George went with Friends to Gracechurch Street Meeting. It was, as usual, a very large and attentive group. Fox stood up and preached an especially long, powerful sermon, "opening many deep and weighty things," according to William Penn.

When he had finished, George knelt and prayed in silence. It was as if he and the congregation knew something very special had happened that day.

Coming out of the meeting house, George turned to one of his companions and remarked that he "felt the cold strike to his heart." But seeing their ashen faces, he added that he was glad he had attended meeting that day. "Now I am clear, I am fully clear," he said. He meant that he had performed his service to God to the fullest of his powers, never holding anything of himself back.

Fox and his companions retired to Friend Henry Gouldney's house in Whitehart Court and spoke more about the excellent meeting that they had just attended. Fox remarked somberly to some of the visitors, "All is well; the Seed of God reigns over all and over death itself." It was his last presentiment.

Fox felt very weak then and had to lie down. Yet he summoned his friends and told them to send various letters to the suffering Quakers, reminding them to "Mind poor Friends in Ireland and America."

Two days later, January 13, he fell asleep peacefully at 9:30 in the evening and never awakened. He was sixty-seven years old.

Penn wrote immediately to Margaret Fox in Swarthmore, but it was too great a distance for her to come in time for the funeral.

The memorial service was attended by several thousand people. Accounts vary from 2,000 to 4,000. The

Meeting House was filled to overflowing and late-com-ers crowded the courtyard. Fox's body was laid in the burying grounds near Bunhill Fields where it is still marked by a modest stone.

After Fox died, it was William Penn who authored the finest epitaph of all. He wrote: "So full of assur-ance was he, that he triumphed over death." It was a fitting tribute to the man who, in life, had triumphed over persecution and imprisonment, over censure and ridicule, and in the end over death itself.

"Many sons have done virtuously in this day," finished Penn, "but dear George, thou excellest them all."

An institution is the lengthened shadow
of one man; as . . . Quakerism, of Fox.
—RALPH WALDO EMERSON

Epilogue
Quakers Today

At George Fox's death, there were some 50,000 Quakers in England and Ireland, out of a population of five million. There were also small groups in Holland, Germany, and America. Fox's Pendle Hill vision of a great multitude, fulfilled within weeks of that spring 1652 vision, continued to grow until today the Society of Friends numbers over 200,000 members, 120,000 of them in the United States, the others in meetings in some thirty-eight different countries.

Quakerism had lifted out of the Puritan movement its purifying value—that of returning to the simple Christianity of the Bible. It had stripped the Protestant churches of their sacramental trappings. It rediscovered the individual mysticism buried in Catholicism and transferred that impulse to the group. In a sense, then, Quakerism became a third form of Christianity, a religious democracy. It was not that the Quakers were presenting something totally new, but that, in Rufus Jones's words, they fused many of the best of the old ideas into "one living truth."

The silent meeting is one of the great gifts that the Quakers have given to organized religion. It is the most easily and universally recognized practice of the Society of Friends. To the Quakers silence is not an end in itself, but a means to the end, which is perfect communion with God. When the priests and professors of the seventeenth century exclaimed: "Look how these people sit mumbing and dumbing! What edification is here where there are no words?" they missed the point of the Quaker silence. It is a full silence, not an empty one.

However, there was a period when even the Quakers seemed to mistake that silence.

After Fox's death, when William and Mary died and gave way first to the reign of Queen Anne and after her the Hanoverian kings, the Quaker "church" solidified. The word "church" is used advisedly, for the Quaker organization that Fox had so carefully constructed had begun to get in the way of the Quaker spirit. In Braithwaite's words, the Society of Friends had become "a state within the State." By 1723, with the death of most of the great Quaker leaders (Barclay, 1690; Fox, 1691; Margaret Fox, 1702; Penn, 1718; George Whitehead, 1723) the first great period of

Quakerism ended. It had been marked by a joyous freedom, great prophetic preaching and fellowship. These were the years when persecution brought the Quakers together so that they could be organized.

The next period of Quakerism was different. The eighteenth century Friends continued along the road that the second-generation Friends had taken. Instead of charging into the eye of the storm as George Fox had always done, the Quakers in the reign of the Georges in England were mainly concerned with preserving and conserving their own quiet way of life. The years of persecution were past. So were the years of conscious discipline. Both persecutions and disciplines had helped turn Quaker meetings into little communities, little preserves, Quaker ghettos. The Quaker Church was no longer willing to go out and save the world.

Again Braithwaite put it best: "When the Georgian years of ease came, they would be years of outward respectability, and inward spiritual decline." These Quakers were more intellectual. They refined Quaker theology and emphasized the homely virtues of diligence and thrift rather than the missionary virtues of zeal and willingness to suffer for the cause.

These Georgian years of ease are often called the "Quietist" period of Quakerism, and it is not an era to which Quaker activists point with any particular pride. Not that anything bad or wicked was done during the Quietist years. But things *not done*, sins of omission rather than commission, still weigh heavily on twentieth century Quaker souls.

John Greenleaf Whittier, the Quaker poet, had this
to say about a typical Friend of the Quietist years:

> With zeal wing-clipped and white-heat cool,
> Moved by the Spirit in grooves of rule,
> No longer harried, and cropped, and fleeced,
> Flogged by sheriff and cursed by priest,
> But by wiser counsels left at ease
> To settle quietly on his lees,
> And, self-concentrated, to count as done
> The work which his fathers well begun,
> In silent protest of letting alone,
> The Quaker kept the way of his own.

It is certainly not a portrait that George Fox or any
of the thousands of imprisoned seventeenth century
Friends might recognize as Quakers. Yet Quakers they
were.

In America, the period of persecutions ended, too,
and Quakers flocked to the New World's shores. To
many who had lost their property in the final years of
harassment in Europe, America was a haven. The
Baptist colony of Rhode Island, always a refuge for religious exiles, welcomed so many Friends that they
soon controlled its politics. In America, unlike England, Friends were always very much aware of the
"outward powers or governments."

New Jersey, purchased in 1674 by Penn and the
Quakers, was colonized by Friends. Burlington, New
Jersey, became the first free Quaker community in
America. Its constitution was an amazing document. It

not only guaranteed freedom of religion, but also insisted on such an innovation as juried trials. It outlawed slavery, capital punishment, and debtor's prison, all things which no self-respecting, seventeenth century colony felt it could do without. Burlington's relations with the Indians were so open that any Indian brought to trial had a jury that consisted of half colonists, half Indians.

In 1682, Penn and hundreds of other Quakers came to America on board *The Welcome*. They settled Pennsylvania, the "Holy Experiment," and drafted the commonwealth's constitution along the same lines as Burlington's. Pennsylvania's treaty with the Indians, according to the French author Voltaire, was "the only treaty never sworn to and never broken." For seventy-five years, until the Quakers resigned control of Pennsylvania because of the French and Indian Wars, the commonwealth was a symbol for religious freedom and friendship.

But in America, as in England, the early fervor gradually disappeared and was replaced by a gathering-in of the Quaker communities. Quakerism became more than a way of worshiping or an ethical approach to life. It became a sharply defined way of living. A cultural pattern emerged that consisted of a written discipline, a dress code, patterns for everyday life. All of these served to distinguish Quakers outwardly— even more than inwardly—from their neighbors.

The plain dress, consisting of bonnets, long dresses of dove gray, and a white scarf folded around the neck for the women, collarless coats in a drab color, broad-brimmed hats for the men, became a badge of identification. At first, in England, plain clothing had been a reaction to the gaudy excesses of Restoration finery where emphasis was on attraction. Quaker dress had been meant for the purpose of *escaping* attention. But it quickly became what it was supposed to fight against —an attention-getting device. As early as 1698, Margaret Fox had mentioned this kind of narrowness as "silly, poor gospel," but it would take until the 1880s in America before plain dress was abandoned.

In America, a pattern peculiar to the New World Quakers emerged, that of "pastoral" meetings. Pastoral meetings are meetings in which ministers preach to a congregation in a regular programed service. Except for some moments of silence before the service, and the fact that there is no ritual of baptism and communion, the pastoral meeting is practically indistinguishable from the neighboring Baptist or Methodist churches.

There is good reason for this. The pastoral meeting sprang up in America in the 1840s in the wide-open country of the Midwest and West. Circuit-riding preachers ministered to far-flung communities, often preaching in a Quaker Meeting House when there was nowhere else to hold services. In such rural communities, an especially good preacher might be asked to stay on. The Quakers were often in the minority in any such church gathering, and gradually became part of the more organized church.

Then, too, in the years after the Civil War, a great
revival movement swept over the Midwest, called the
Wesleyan Revival. Quakers shared in revival meetings, often holding them in their Meeting Houses.
Again, the visiting evangelist would be invited to stay
on. As one Quaker historian writes, "In the space of a
generation, most of the mid-west yearly meetings
adopted the pastoral system."

By the twentieth century in America, there were a
great many and varied ways of being a Friend. Basi-
cally, though, American Friends can be divided into
three approximately equal groups: the silent-meeting
Friends who adhere to the historical Quaker worship;
the pastoral-modernist Friends who are in the mainstream of American Protestantism; and the pastoral-
fundamentalists who are Biblical literalists.

When most people today think of Quakers, they
think of pacifists, that is, people who are utterly opposed to war for any reason. They identify the essence
of Quakerism with the declaration Fox wrote in 1661,
renouncing "all outward wars and strife and fightings
with outward weapons for any end or under any pretense whatever."

While it is true that the Quakers hold that war is
wrong, it is not true that all Quakers are pacifists. Indeed, even in the beginning, many of the first convinced Friends were soldiers. They remained soldiers
until they, themselves, were certain that they should
put away their weapons. No one told them that they

had to do so to remain Quakers. Fox put it, "Let no Friends go beyond their own measure given them of God. . . ."

Still it was always important that Friends be reminded of the Light Within as the group saw it. The Quakers held that if a man or woman was truly faithful to the Light Within, he or she would come to the inescapable conclusion that war—for "any pretense whatever"—was wrong. It was in this mood that representatives of many meetings went in 1971 to Washington to stand silently in front of the White House to remind Quaker president, Richard M. Nixon, that he had not seen clearly in regard to the Indo-China war.

If the silent meeting is the most easily recognized practice of the Friends Meeting and pacifism the belief most often associated with the Quakers, surely the American Friends Service Committee (the AFSC as it is often called) is the organization most people think of when they think about Quakers. Yet this organization is not an old one at all. It was organized in 1917 for reconstruction work in France by conscientious objectors to the war—"a service of love in wartime," is how they put it. There is an older similar organization among British Friends, the Friends Service Council. The AFSC and the Friends Service Council are always in the thick of Quaker activist activities, or Quaker "outreach" as it is called.

This "outreach" is a direct result of the Quaker concept of personal "concern," where individuals, moved to action by the plight of others, asked both the blessings and material support of their Monthly or Yearly Meetings. The AFSC is organized outreach. For example, it engages in every kind of war relief and takes no sides in any war. It has helped both German and French sufferers of World War II, both North and South Vietnamese victims, both Arab and Jewish refugees. At the same time, the AFSC is very active in all forms of draft counseling, promoting international and interracial understanding, running peace institutes, aiding the underprivileged everywhere.

Just as the nineteenth century Quakers were the backbone of the abolitionist and antislavery movements, the organizers of the underground railroad that delivered hundreds of black men and women out of slavery in America, so the modern Quakers in the AFSC (and through the AFSC) fight for the rights of people enslaved by prejudice and poverty the world around. The eight-pointed red-and-black star of the Quaker service organizations has become a symbol of hope and help throughout the world. In 1947, the AFSC and the Friends Service Council in London together won the Nobel Peace Prize.

The experience of three centuries of Quakerism has led to some modifications in both the spirit and the system, but the essential features and many of the details of both spirit and system that Fox preached in the 1600s are unchanged.

And most important, the concept of the Inner Light, or as George Fox said 300 years ago: "I live, yet not I, but Christ in me," is what endures. It is the Quaker gift to the world.

Bibliography

TITLES MARKED WITH AN ASTERISK ARE ESPECIALLY FOR
YOUNG READERS.

Allott, Stephen, *Quaker Pioneers*. London: Bannisdale Press,
 1963.

"Beliefs and Practices of the American Friends Service
 Committee," AFSC reprint.

Braithwaite, William C., *Beginnings of Quakerism*. London:
 Macmillan, 1921.

————, *The Second Period of Quakerism*. London: Cambridge
 University Press, 1961.

Brayshaw, A. Neave, *The Quakers*. London: George Allen
 and Unwin, Ltd., 1921.

Brinton, Howard, "The Society of Friends." Wallingford,
 Pa.: Pendle Hill Pamphlet #48.

———, "Quakerism and Other Religions." Wallingford, Pa.: Pendle Hill Pamphlet #93.

———, "The Religion of George Fox." Wallingford, Pa.: Pendle Hill Pamphlet #161.

———, *Friends for 300 Years*. Philadelphia: Pendle Hill Pamphlets, 1952, 1964.

Bronner, Edwin B., editor, *American Quakers Today*. Philadelphia: Friends World Committee, 1966.

Cadbury, Henry J., *Quakerism and Early Christianity*. London: George Allen and Unwin, Ltd., 1957.

Churchill, Winston S., *Marlborough: His Life and Times*. New York: Charles Scribner's Sons, 1968.

* Elgin, Kathleen, *The Quakers*. New York: David McKay, 1968.

Fox, George, *George Fox's Journal*. Edited by Rufus M. Jones. Capricorn Books Edition. New York: G. P. Putnam's Sons, 1963.

———, *Journal*. Edited by Norman Penney. Everyman Edition. New York: E. P. Dutton, Inc., 1924.

Hayes, John Russell, *Old Meeting Houses*. Philadelphia: Biddle Press, 1909.

Hoyland, Geoffrey, "The Use of Silence." Wallingford, Pa.: Pendle Hill Pamphlet #83.

*Jones, Rufus M., *The Story of George Fox*. Philadelphia: Friends Book Store, 1943.

———, *Spiritual Reformers in the 16th and 17th Centuries*. Boston: Beacon Press, 1959.

Kenworthy, Leonard S., *Quaker Leaders Speak*. Philadelphia: Friends Book Store, 1952.

King, Rachel Hadley, *George Fox and the Light Within*. Philadelphia: Grant, 1940.

Lyttle, Brad, "National Defense Thru Nonviolent Resistance." Chicago: Shahn-Ti Pub., 1959.

Market Bosworth District Council, "Market Bosworth, Official Guide."

Norlind, Emelia Fogelklou, "The Atonement of George Fox." Wallingford, Pa.: Pendle Hill Pamphlet #166.

Peare, Catherine Owens, *William Penn*. Ann Arbor: University of Michigan Press, 1956.

Tolles, Frederick B., and Alderfer, E. Gordon, editors, *The Witness of William Penn*. New York: The Macmillan Company, 1957.

* Van Etten, Henry, *George Fox and the Quakers*. New York: Harper Torchbooks, Harper & Row, 1959.

Wildes, Harry Emerson, *Voice of the Lord*. Philadelphia: University of Pennsylvania Press, 1965.

Wilson, Gladys, *Quaker Worship*. London: Bannisdale Press, 1952.

Index

Act of Uniformity (1662), 111, 114
Adamites, 44
Aldam, Thomas, 73, 124
American Friends Service Committee, 171–72
Anglicanism, 13
Audland, John, 50, 51
Authority, *see* Scriptural authority

Barclay, Robert, 125
Bennett, Gervase, 39, 40
Berkley, Lord, 152–53
Bibles, 12, 14, 15
Boleyn, Anne, 10, 11
Burrough, Edward, 51, 65, 111
Business meetings, 125–27

Camm, John, 51
Camm, Thomas, 58, 73
Catherine of Aragon, 10–11
Catholicism, 10–14, 75, 159
Caton, William, 124

Ceely, Peter, 77–78, 84–86
"Center down," 5
Charles I, King of England, 14, 16, 40, 68, 70
Charles II, King of England, 100, 102–11, 123, 131–32, 159
Children of the Light, 51, 65, 70
Churchill, John, 159
Churches, *see* Steeple-houses
Clarendon Code, 112
Clayton, Ann, 143
Community, 96
Conventicle Act (1664), 112, 114, 132, 148–49
Corbett, Thomas, 152
Cradock, Dr., 20
Cromwell, Oliver, 40–41, 68–75, 98–100, 102, 116–17
Crosslands, Sir Jordan, 123
Crowther, Joseph, 150
Curtis, Ann, 105

Declaration of Breda (1660), 102, 103
Diggers, 44
Doomsdale, 86–88
Dress, 168–69
Drury, Captain, 71, 72
Dyer, Mary, 110

Easton, Nicholas, 143
Edward VI, King of England, 13
Elizabeth I, Queen of England, 13–14
English Protestant Church, 11, 14
Equality of women, 27–28, 153–54
Erbury, Dorcas, 89

Farnsworth, Richard, 51, 56, 57, 154
Fell, George, 129, 131
Fell, Margaret Askew, 52–59, 65, 72, 98, 104–5, 109–10, 114–18, 128–32, 134, 136–37, 148–49, 151–52, 160, 162, 169
Fell, Thomas, 52–53, 56–58, 60–61, 98–99
Fifth Monarchy Men, 108–10
Folkingham, Nicholas, 31
Forstall, Richard, 140
Forster, Thomas, 138–39
Fox, Christopher, 7, 67
Fox, George
    appearance of, 45–46, 78
    arrests and imprisonments of, 31–41, 63–64, 71, 76–87, 103–5, 108–10, 114–23, 148–52
    birth of, 8
    death of, 161–63
    education of, 8–10
    faults of, 19, 23, 40, 46, 61
    illnesses of, 101–2, 134–35, 140–41
    magic and, 48–49, 139
    marriage of, 59, 128–31
    ministry of, 22–32
    old age of, 158–61
    personality of, 17–18
    presentiments of, 99–100, 148, 162
    speech of, 46–47
    strength of, 29, 48
    travels of, 18–20, 97, 127–28, 137–46
    visions of, 18, 21, 42–43, 49–50, 120
    writing of, 47, 83–84, 135, 156–57
Fox, Margaret, see Fell, Margaret Askew
Fox, Mary Lagos, 7–9, 151
Friends Service Council, 171, 172

Gee, George, 9, 16, 17
Gibran, Kahlil, 5
Glynne, John, 82–86
Gouldney, Henry, 162

Hacker, Francis, 70–71
Hat controversy, 45–46
Henrietta Maria, Queen of England, 14, 16, 40, 68
Henry VIII, King of England, 10–12
Hooton, Elizabeth, 25, 138, 141
Howgill, Francis, 50, 51, 65, 73

Indians, 142, 145–46
Industry (ship), 137–40
Inner Light, 26, 31, 34, 56, 90, 91, 95, 96, 123, 145

James I, King of England, 14
James II, King of England, 159–60, 161
Jones, Rufus, 51, 126

Keate, John, 80–81
Kirkby, Colonel, 114–15, 129, 160

Lampitt, William, 53–54, 57
Leddra, William, 110
Light within, see Inner Light
Lower, Thomas, 148–50, 152, 156
Luther, Martin, 10, 15

Marche, Edward, 109, 123
Marriage, Quaker, 130
Mary I, Queen of England, 13
Mary II, Queen of England, 161

Monmouth, Duke of, 159
Monthly Meetings, 125–26

Nayler, James, 51, 56–57, 89–96, 101, 124, 134, 153–54
Nixon, Richard M., 171
Nobel Prize, 172

Oath of Abjuration, 75, 76, 78, 84, 99
Oath taking, 30, 75, 117–20

Pacifism, 73, 104–5, 170–71
Parker, Justice, 150
Parnell, James, 96
Parr, Catherine, 11
Pastoral meeting, 169–70
Penington, Isaac, 145
Penn, William, 8, 14–15, 35, 46, 58, 66–67, 124, 130–31, 146, 148, 152, 162–63, 167–68
Perrot, John, 153, 154
Pickering, Edward, 19
Plain language, 47
Priests, 15, 18–22
Prison reform, 41
Professors, 17–18, 22
Puritans, 14, 99, 101
Pyot, Edward, 77, 78, 80, 89

Quakers, origin of name, 39

Ranters, 43
Reckless, John, 33–34
Roberts, Gerrard, 134–35
Robinson, William, 110

Sands, Captain, 56
Sawrey, John, 55, 56, 60, 62
Schisms, 153–57
Scriptural authority, 31, 36, 62
"Seed, The," 26, 124–36
Seekers, 20, 49–51
Sharman, Thomas, 38–39
Silence, 3–6, 9–10, 165
Simonds, Martha, 89, 91
Slavery, 141, 172
Social reform, 29–30
Society of Bristol (ship), 146
Society of Friends, 25, 126
Steeple-houses, 25, 28, 30
Stephens, Nathaniel, 67
Stephenson, Marmaduke, 110
Stoddard, Amos, 26
Story, John, 153–57
Stranger, Hannah, 89–92
Swearing, see Oath taking
Sylvester, Nathaniel, 144

Threshing meetings, 65
Toleration Act (1689), 161
Tyndale, William, 12

Violence, 34–35, 101

West, William, 61–62
Whitehead, George, 109
Whittier, John Greenleaf, 167
Wilkinson, John, 153–57
William of Orange, 161
Williams, Roger, 144
Women, equality of, 27–28, 153–54
Wycliffe, John, 12